Social and Personal Identity

Social and Personal Identity

Understanding Your*Self*

Derek Layder

SAGE Publications
London • Thousand Oaks • New Delhi

First published 2004

 SAGE Publications Ltd
1 Oliver's Yard
55 City Road
London EC1Y 1SP

SAGE Publications Inc.
2455 Teller Road
Thousand Oaks, California 91320

SAGE Publications India Pvt Ltd
B-42, Panchsheel Enclave
Post Box 4109
New Delhi 100 017

British Library Cataloguing in Publication data

A catalogue record for this book is available
from the British Library

ISBN 0-7619-4488-5
     0-7619-4489-3

Library of Congress control number available

Typeset by C&M Digitals (P) Ltd, Chennai, India
Printed in Great Britain by Athenaeum Press, Gateshead

Contents

Introduction

How much do you know about yourself? Do you know why some people and experiences make you feel frustrated and unhappy while others leave you feeling elated and energized? Do you feel that life is exciting and challenging, or do you think it's mostly a drag, full of unnecessary rules, restrictions and problems? Do you get on well with your parents, your mates, your boyfriend or girlfriend? Or do your relationships constantly provide you with headaches and heartaches?

How sensitive are you? Can you tell when your partner is in need of tender loving care, or do they have to make a big scene before you catch on? What are the greatest lows in your life, what are the greatest joys – and why do you see them this way? Do you think you have changed over the years – your general attitudes, your responses to other people and your self-image? These are the kinds of questions and issues dealt with in this book. As an introduction to the topic of social and personal identity it will help you understand yourself and the kinds of problems that you experience in daily life.

It does so by explaining what the self or personal identity is, and how it is supported or undermined by common social experiences, personal problems, and the quality of your relationships. It enables you to put your own identity in perspective and helps you understand why some of your experiences are negative while others are life enhancing. By providing you with an understanding of personal identity in general it allows you to gain insight into your own personal world and how you can gain more from your experiences.

Emotion and personal identity

Although each of us is profoundly influenced by our surrounding society and social relationships, we are also unique individuals. We respond to life's problems and circumstances quite differently from anyone else. This capacity is a reflection of our personal identity and allows us to experience life in a way that is distinct from others. It enables us to have our own unique 'take' on the world.

However, the conflict between having to conform with what is expected of us, but also wanting to do this in our own way often makes us feel at odds with ourselves, with other people or even social institutions like school and work. Personal identity is always caught up in, and constantly emerges from, this tension between fitting in with society and other people (especially those with whom we are intimate) and wanting to follow our own desires, hopes and wishes.

This book outlines a view of personal and social identity that emphasizes the way in which we, as individuals, make sense of our own experiences. Each of us has different levels and types of awareness and perception – practical, emotional, self-protective and so on – that shape our views of ourselves, the world and other people. This allows us to respond to situations and problems in terms of our own unique sense of who we are, usually in a manner that offers the 'best' side of ourselves to other people. Of course, things don't always go well, or at least in the way we anticipate and as a result, this unintentionally contributes to life's 'rich tapestry'.

The problem is that we are all emotionally needy but each of us has different patterns of need. We all require a certain amount of love, care and attention. We need to feel we belong, that we are accepted, that we are valued and that other people need us as much as we need them. That is, a basic level of need must be met in order for us to feel self-confident, and secure about dealing with other people and life's problems. However, the balance in our needs and desires shifts constantly both in terms of long-term personal development as well as in relation to everyday problems and events.

We must have a basic level of inner security otherwise we wouldn't be able to do anything properly, but at various times we also feel pangs of insecurity. The extent of the insecurity is the key. We might feel insecure about whether we are loveable, whether we have enough confidence, our ability to make things happen, or to turn bad circumstances around. Usually such feelings are short-lived and only occur in certain situations, such as going on a first date with someone, or attending a job interview. However, some individuals live their whole lives in state of chronic insecurity that restricts their ability to do things and to enjoy themselves to the fullest extent. Why is this?

Your controlling heart

To enjoy a satisfying life you must be able to translate your wishes, hopes, desires and needs into reality. This requires that you are able to manage and deal with other people so that they naturally provide you with the things you need most, whatever they may be: love, companionship, attention, care, a sense of purpose, feelings of elation and joy and so on. To accomplish this, you have to sensitively 'read' other people for their moods, attitudes and preferences and then act upon this information in a way that meshes with your own needs and desires. Of course this isn't a one-way street. You cannot afford to be totally selfish otherwise people will refuse to co-operate.

An important rule of social life here, is that of reciprocity. You must offer something back in exchange for what you desire. But for true personal satisfaction there has to be more than mere exchange. There must be genuine emotional commitment to the other person. You must take account of their interests, wishes, needs and desires in the way that you deal with them. In short, you must be able to benignly control, influence and direct the other people in your life so that they satisfy your emotional needs and desires while, at the same time, they satisfy their own by doing the same with you. In this sense the smooth working of personal relationships depends on mutual benign control.

Of course, much of social life is not smooth and trouble free. This is because the delicate balancing involved in mutual benign control often breaks down either abruptly, or through slow deterioration. When this happens the essential empathy, care and mutual co-operation of benign influence becomes displaced by selfishness, and manipulation. Emotional blackmail is a common example of such psychological manipulation. The blackmailer says, in effect, 'if I don't get my way and you don't comply, then I'll withdraw my love, care and support for you'. An ultimatum like this may seem effective in the short term, but since it is based on emotional manipulation, it often produces a brittle and merely outward show of consent in its human 'target'.

Experiencing life and personal identity

Many relationship problems hinge around the conflict between the need for aloneness (independence, personal space) and the desire for togetherness (involvement and doing things with others). This mirrors the tension between the individualism that accompanies personal identity and the pressure towards 'fitting-in' or social conformity, mentioned earlier. Intimate relationships often get into trouble because the partners find it difficult to adjust to each other's needs with regard to personal space and independence.

Sometimes this is because one partner doesn't recognize the other's feelings, for example, of being too hemmed-in, or smothered. More seriously, as far as the future of the relationship is concerned, trouble may arise because your own security is threatened by the thought of allowing your partner more freedom and independence. Such problems and dilemmas highlight our personal responsibility for who we are, how we live our lives and how we behave towards others. It also stresses that the burden of such responsibility is not something that we can necessarily take for granted.

Being able to participate competently, smoothly and satisfyingly in personal relationships and in social life generally is a skilled accomplishment and requires a great deal of effort, energy and ingenuity. But regardless of how much energy and enthusiasm you expend, unless you employ the skills of benign control (including emotional intelligence) you will fall short in creating really satisfying relationships.

There are other reasons why 'complete' satisfaction may remain elusive. The point of benign control is to get others to willingly cater for your needs and desires and not simply to make them comply. This requires gentle forms of persuasion and 'seduction' in which they are free to reject or alter any arrangement they may enter into with you. Without doubt, the unpredictability of others, the incompleteness of our influence over them, and not really knowing what will happen next, are necessary for generating ongoing excitement in relationships. Thus the uncertainty we often feel in relationships is double edged; it may produce anxiety, but it can also offer an irresistible frisson.

It is also true that we are all imperfect beings who are humanly flawed. No matter how unselfish and caring you may try to be, inevitably there will be times when your own interests and desires will be your most important concern, or when someone else's interests directly override yours. In this respect our lives and relationships always elude our attempts at (complete) control. Perhaps we should face up to the brutal fact that we will always be trying to make things a little better or more satisfying than they are.

The key to a positive experience of personal identity is how you respond to the trials and tribulations of life, be they trivial, everyday upsets or more serious misfortunes such as debilitating illness, or the ending of an important relationship. In order to combat set backs, or bounce back from such misfortunes you require personal resilience, self-belief and a dogged determination to overcome the forces that stand in the way of personal happiness. Your ability to do so depends in large part on how much personal security and self-esteem you already have in the bank, so to speak.

Whether you succumb to depression and pessimism, or become defeated and resigned to failure, is strongly influenced by the strength of personal identity, its stability and your ability to act effectively. A solid sense of who you are and a strong urge to overcome adversity is enough to transform a defeatist attitude into one keen to turn things around. But often the problems and trials of life have a cumulative effect on energy reserves and your will to carry on and push through difficult times. Mental health, in this respect, is always delicately balanced around the interplay of personal identity and social circumstances.

Becoming who you are

Your personal and social identity is never static, but this doesn't mean you are constantly revising who you are according to how you feel. Just because you adopt a new fashion style or a 'cooler' way of talking doesn't mean that your personal and social identity has substantially changed. These are purely cosmetic or outer changes and more likely reflect other aspects of yourself (your sub-personae), than to truly indicate a change in core self-identity.

In terms of longer-term personal growth, changes in personal identity are more often gradual and incremental than abrupt and 'total' makeovers. In this sense personal identity is constantly changing in a way that isn't necessarily obvious. But neither does it change simply because we are tired of our current self-image and want to try something new. Personal and social identity is not like that. Of course we always have images of, and ideas about the sort of person we would like to be, or become and sometimes try hard to make them real.

It is also true that in the final analysis it is you and you alone who is responsible for the kind of person you are, the way you live your life, and how you treat others. No one else can be you, or live your life for you. But it is not true that you can change your identity on a whim, or by an act of will. Any such attempt would either be purely theatrical, and hence inauthentic, or in order to deceive and manipulate others. In neither case could we say that identity change was genuine.

Real changes in personal identity emerge out of the creative interplay between social circumstances and events and the way you as an individual respond to them. No matter how assertive or dominant a personality you are, in the final instance your identity needs to be grounded in social reality. Other people have to accept you as you yourself wish to be accepted before your personal desire for change will have any bite or social validation.

Using this book

This book is designed to give you a thorough introduction to the topic of social and personal identity and as such helps you gain fresh insights into yourself. It allows you to understand what makes you tick, how you relate to others and how you feel about yourself, the world and life in general. It reveals how your moods and general mental well-being are dependent on the balance of your emotionally-based needs and desires, as well as your ability to enlist others' empathy, care and support.

It provides a clear understanding of the dynamics of personal and social identity and the manner in which they are shaped by the social world. It also offers a view of personal identity as emotionally saturated and intimately linked with personal experience and social relationships. The book gives an account of personal and social identity that you will not necessarily find in other 'textbooks'. I've tried to write it not as a textbook in the usual sense, but as one that is hopefully readable and engaging because it deals with identity in the context of real issues in the real world of personal experience.

I'd like to thank Martyn Denscombe and Ian Burkitt for reading and commenting on an earlier draft of this book. Both of them offered me excellent and constructive advice about various matters that I found invaluable in completing the final draft. Although having no direct bearing on the practical issues of writing, others have indirectly influenced some of the ideas that appear in it. Charles and Olive Jones may not be aware of it, but they inspired some of my thoughts on the nature of interpersonal ethics in everyday life. I thank them for it, as I do my sister Brenda Layder, without whom Charles' and Olive's influence might not have reached me in the first place.

1

Understanding Your*Self*

Chapter Preview

- The five essential dimensions of self-identity.
- The inner organization of the self; levels and types of awareness.
- The self as a unifying centre of emotional need, consciousness and executive capacities.

In short and simple terms the 'self' or 'personal identity' is how a person regards themselves and how they, and others, relate to, or behave towards themselves. Put slightly more formally the self is a centre of awareness, emotional needs and desires, in terms of which an individual reflects and acts upon his or her social circumstances. To understand the more complex issues involved it is useful to distinguish three aspects of the self. They are: its general attributes, its internal organization and the needs, functions and capacities of the self (see Figure 1.1).

The self has five principal dimensions or properties. First, I'll outline these in brief and then discuss them in greater detail.

1   The self is both social *and* psychological in nature, it is neither exclusively psychological or social. Something of the self always stands apart from the social world. At the same time the self can only exist *within* a social context.
2   The self is essentially emotional in nature. Although people are knowledgeable, skilful and rational, these capacities must be understood as closely allied to emotions.
3   The self is a centre of awareness, executive agency and control over self and others. It is capable of different types and intensities of control ranging from gentle benign control and influence to extreme exploitation and coercion.
4   The self is flexible and pliable in two major senses. First, at any one point in time it may manifest itself in different (and sometimes contradictory),

Figure 1.1   Components of the complex self

guises. Second, over time, the self changes, evolves and develops. In this sense it is part of an emergent narrative of self-realization.

5   The self has a spiritual aspect which often remains undeveloped and dormant. Everyone has the potential for developing what has been referred to as a 'higher self'. This is not inevitable and requires sensitivity, commitment and 'education'. It may develop as part of a process of personal development or 'self-transformation'.

Self in society and society in self

No one can stand apart from the social world. Everyone is influenced by society and it makes its indelible mark on us. It's a great error to think that there is no such thing as society or that we are separate, self-sufficient individuals. Everyone is influenced by family, friends, education, ethnicity, work, class, gender, politics and history. At every point in our lives we both rely on, and contribute to our social environment.

On the one hand, we can never be 'outside' society and its tentacles, but on the other we (our behaviour thoughts and feelings) are not simply formed or determined by society. We have a unique 'inner' self which chooses what to do and how to do it. Often, these two ideas – that we are 'inside' society at the same time as standing 'apart from it' – are thought to be incompatible. But this is not true. They are not only compatible, but go together naturally in social life.

Although we can never stand completely apart from society, we nevertheless retain a certain amount of independence from it. We are able to choose how we behave towards others in ways that are, for us 'appropriate' and that satisfy our own needs, wishes and desires. Society can only present us with a set of choices, it can never completely determine for us which choices we actually adopt. Of course, social pressures, to conform, or fit in with established patterns of behaviour always constrain us to some extent (this varies according to different issues and situations). However, there is always a private, personal space in which we are free to choose for ourselves and to be self-responsible, if we so wish. In this sense we carry around in our heads whole chunks of society's influence, in the form of rules, regulations, laws, fashion, advertising images, expectations about how others will behave towards us and so on. These inevitably inform our choices and decisions, but we are free to make up our own minds about whether they are applicable or relevant to us and the situations in which we find ourselves. Very often, we simply use these as guidelines and invent our own 'versions' of them. This is because of two characteristics.

First, we are self-directing beings capable of independent thought and behaviour. We have the knowledge and skills that allow us to deal with other people and situations in our own terms. We are not completely trapped by our circumstances – unless we wish to be, or if we refuse to fight against them. We may be 'trapped' in poverty, but we can choose how we will respond to it, either by resigned acceptance, or by a fierce determination not to be a victim. In the end, we may only be able to transform 'our situation' a tiny bit. This may simply amount to being satisfied with the fact that we've made an effort, rather than feeling defeated or resentful because we couldn't do more. Alternatively, the change we are able to make may be a minor way of making our lives, or our neighbours lives, a little more comfortable. Nevertheless, 'minor' change, is change!

Second, we are all unique individuals because we have all had a unique set of experiences. Even if you were brought up in the same family, you experience the world in different ways than your brothers or sisters. Their disappointments or their joys were never exactly the same as yours. The way you responded to important events was different from theirs. We each experience a unique configuration of events, turning points, as well as the feelings and behavioural responses which accompany them, as we develop through childhood, adolescence and adulthood. Our unique experiences, have made us into unique persons with our distinct personalities and abilities, our particular behavioural styles, our diverse moods and sensitivities. We each have our own distinctive ways of reacting to events, or of relating to people.

Both these characteristics then, ensure that we are never simply at the mercy of social forces. At the same time, we ourselves are never completely free from social influences. We are always making choices *with regard to* the social circumstances in which we find ourselves. Our private space or personal 'bubble' is forever fenced in by the limits of our social environment. So we exist inside society while society resides inside us, our brains, our memories and our experiences. Society though, is always in part 'outside' us at the same time. Our relationships with our friends, family and work colleagues, impersonal government bureaucracies, stretch away from, and beyond us as individuals. Similarly, social organizations and institutions in a wider sense, have a 'life of their own' independent of any one of us as individuals. Just as we as individuals have a personal space which we defend from the intrusions of society and its influence.

The fact that we have a foot in both psychological reality and social reality is reflected in the tension between what I refer to as the duality of separateness and relatedness (Layder 1997). The self is always caught up in some aspect of this tension – between having a life 'apart' from others and being involved with and dependent (although not over-dependent) on others. It is difficult for us as individuals to come to a satisfactory resolution of this problem, since every time we express a desire to be alone, or have some space of our own, we are automatically rejecting the idea of togetherness and involvement. Conversely, when we commit to others, in some part, we surrender our autonomy and independence.

Nevertheless, this duality persists in many forms in social life and I shall have occasion to describe the diferent ways in which it affects the self. In particular, Chapters 6 and 7 explore the diverse 'dilemmas' of behaviour that are posed for us in everday life and which stem from this basic duality. In this sense the fact that we exist in both psychological and social reality, is a mirror image of the tension between our existence as separate (autonomous) individuals, and the fact that we cannot exist outside the encompassing envelope of society and social relations.

The emotional self

We are emotional beings. We frequently hold certain feelings in check, but at other times it is almost impossible not to let them out. Although many of us are reluctant to talk about our emotions or deepest feelings (and this applies as much to women as it does men), they always influence our thoughts and behaviour. We aren't simply detached, calculating creatures who weigh up the pros and cons of our actions before we do anything. More often than not, our personal commitments, feelings and values are directly involved in our dealings and relationships with others.

The self isn't just a body with a brain attached to it. Of course, our bodies and brains are important, but they are merely the starting point. More significantly, we have an inner mental life which allows us to reflect on our responses to others, and their's on us. This inner life is rich with emotional freight (feelings, attitudes, stored memories – good and bad – and so on), which feeds into our behaviour, sometimes deliberately and sometimes, unintentionally. This emotional part of our nature is all too often overlooked or its importance is denied – in everyday life, and in academic social analysis.

Emotions and the motivations to which they give rise have frequently been denied any important role in our day-to-day conduct by even the most sophisticated of social theorists. Anthony Giddens, for example, is of the view that emotions and motives are not directly involved in everyday human behaviour. Instead, what he calls 'reflexive monitoring' and 'rationalization' (reason giving and rational understanding) play the major roles. Motives only play a part in 'relatively unusual circumstances, situations which in some way break the routine' (Giddens 1984, p. 6). Even when it does play a role, 'unconscious' motivation (as in Freud's work) is more important than anything of which we are consciously aware. My view of the emotions and motivation is the exact opposite of Giddens'. The feelings that motivate us do not simply derive from a deep unconscious in a Freudian sense. Although they are often below the level of current 'awareness' this is frequently because we try to deny or suppress them. Otherwise they remain 'subconscious' – outside the range of present-moment awareness – because they are not necessary for the tasks immediately at hand. Indeed, in this sense they may stay out of our conscious awareness for years.

Similarly, although we always use our cognitive skills to give reasons for what we say and do, they are in no sense more important than, or separate from our feelings, motivations and emotions. In fact, 'reflexive monitoring' and the 'rationalization' of conduct are soaked through with emotions and feelings. Our plans, purposes and intentions – our motivations – enter directly into, and underpin our everyday behaviour, they don't simply refer to the *potential* for action, as Giddens insists.

To exclude emotion and motivation from rational thought and cognition creates a false division between them which must be broken down. All human behaviour is suffused by feelings, emotions and motives and as a consequence they flood into, and deeply influence our 'rationalizations' and 'reflexive monitoring'. Because they enter into behaviour directly and diffusely, emotion and motivation are massively present in routine day-to-day conduct as well as unusual and non-routine circumstances. They are certainly not restricted to the small space of 'exceptional circumstances' as Giddens would have us believe.

Many social scientists and psychologists have either denied or subordinated the influence of the emotions by claiming that we humans are basically 'rational actors' and that feelings and emotions are simply 'tag-ons' to these more significant factors. In this account we think and behave in an efficient, logical and calculating fashion designed to maximize our satisfaction (the emotional reward). Moreover, these writers believe that to behave on the basis of how you feel emotionally is to be irrational (illogical, inefficient and impractical). But patently, we do not live our lives simply according to some practical calculus. The fact that we always let our feelings have a role in what we do, doesn't mean we are being 'irrational'.

To call someone irrational in this sense, is an attempt to discredit them. But it is a mistake to confuse the influence of our feelings with being 'irrational'. If we love someone it is surely 'rational' to trust them. If we are afraid of someone it is rational to avoid or be wary of them. Without doubt, our reflective intelligence is constantly at work as we steer our way through daily encounters. It is not a question of denying the importance of rationality, logic and so on in our behaviour. However, feelings, like love, fear, disapproval, envy, empathy and so on play an equally important role.

The emotional or feeling side of our nature goes hand in hand with our reflective, intelligent and calculating side. In most instances the different strands are mixed together in different proportions. But in some instances one strand may predominate over the others, as in the stuffy rule-bound bureaucrat or the child, open-mouthed and filled with wonderment. No behaviour though, is completely empty of emotion, although its importance often goes unrecognized or supressed. The ever-presence of emotion (including what Goleman 1996 calls 'emotional intelligence') may, therefore, prompt us to reconsider our daily encounters. For instance, from the 'outside' people's conversations often seem to go smoothly and well, with everyone enjoying shared understanding, attention and feeling. But on closer inspection they turn out to be full of 'errors', misunderstandings, and confusion (a 'fast moving blur' as Scheff 1990, describes it).

Sometimes we even feel strangely 'apart' from the conversation, or somehow not right, not included or awkward (Turner 1988). This is because on one level we are usually listening to what the other person is saying, while at the same time we are feeling and thinking 'other' things that remain unsaid. So even though we may nod in agreement with someone and say 'sure!' or 'absolutely', we may actually be feeling totally out of kilter with them. You may diasgree with them vehemently, but prefer not to get into an argument or fight.

Another reason for this lack of attunement, is that we often 'deceive' ourselves as well as others (or at least mislead them) so as to avoid anything we might find embarrassing from occurring in the conversation. In this sense much of our personal behaviour seeks feelings of well-being, pride, and self-confidence while avoiding feelings of embarrassment, shame, insecurity and so on. To this end we try to enlist the help and support of others by convincing them, or conveying the impression, that indeed we are confident, proud, trustworthy, etc.

So there are different levels at which we communicate with others, and this is, in no small way, the result of emotion and feeling. Very often we are not completely aware of the feelings that underpin our seemingly 'more rational' decisions, statements or actions. Talk about emotions is frequently avoided, or their existence and influence is denied. Nevertheless, emotion is everywhere and ever-present in our lives. In this respect it shadows another facet of daily life and social interaction; power and personal control. Emotions and control are two sides of the same coin.

The controlling self

Neither our emotional nor calculative side is ever able to have free rein over our thoughts and behaviour. This is because there is a continual need to have some control over ourselves and other people. Being 'out-of-control', or not having enough control in certain areas, can seriously damage personal relationships and can prevent us from leading satisfying and fulfilling lives. To understand the role of control in your life, you have to appreciate its 'lighter' side, which has been, and continues to be, almost totally ignored while its 'darker' side gets all the attention. This 'lighter' side includes gentler, more caring and sociable aspects and is closely mixed in with our feelings and emotions. In this sense personal control is linked to desire and the need for intimacy.

We all have basic psychological (and emotional) needs for love, acceptance and approval (among others) and it is true that, at least in part, these may be met by drawing on our own resources. Thus, it has become something of a commonplace to acknowledge that self-love, self-acceptance and self-approval, are all essential constituents of a person's health, happiness and mental adjustment. However, unfortunately this is not enough. We also need others to care for us, to approve of us and to 'believe' in us in order that our own self-attitudes and feelings may be maintained. Thus, these psychological needs are simultaneously social needs. Only lovers, friends, family, work colleagues and so on, can supply us with these.

We require some means of 'producing' or creating these responses to us. We need to be able to attract others to us and to entice or encourage them to bestow upon us their love, care, acceptance. One principal way of encouraging others to do this is to offer them something in return, either before or after they offer something to us. In this manner we engage in a sort of mutual exchange of gifts or offerings which allow us all to benefit. Take love for instance. Romantic love works best when the two people involved love each other to the same extent. Each of the lovers will reaffirm their intimate bond by giving each other little gifts or symbols of affection, such as kisses, presents, hugs, being thoughful, not taking each other for granted and so on. They will continue to do this as long as each remains in love with the other and as long as certain agreed conditions are met, such as being faithful to each other. But, if the reciprocity breaks down and the partners begin to feel less satisfied because the balance of power has changed, this will pose a threat to the relationship. It may not necessarily mean the end of the relationship, but unless mutually satisfying adjustments are made, then this may well signal an eventual unhappy ending. This highlights the fact that each person needs to feel as though they have some control over the relationship – control over what happens to them and their partner, as well as control over the kind of feelings this creates – happiness, bliss, insecurity, domination and so forth.

Unless we feel we have some control, then we will be uncomfortable, unhappy and seek to leave or change the situation. (Of course, it may not always be possible to leave, but this doesn't prevent us from wanting to leave.) This applies to all social relationships, at all stages, and not just to romantic love. Whether we can succesfully manage our relationships and achieve our desires, will depend on our personal power and the kind of situation we are in. In order to be loved we need to convince at least one other person to love us. And to do this we need whatever personal resources we have, such as physical attraction, personal magnetism, being good at conversations and so forth, to count for us in a positive sense.

If you're unable to attract others in this way (perhaps even, have quite the opposite effect), then this will eventually undermine your confidence and self-esteem and hence decrease your personal power. Often people suffering from depression and anxiety, or even more serious mental ill-health have suffered from the experience of a 'draining-away' of power and control like this (Gilbert 1992). Clearly, good mental health requires that we have some control over ourselves, our lives, as well as over other people.

The fact that we are dependent on each other in society reinforces the importance of mutual exchanges (of gifts and offerings) and the messages they convey. Social interaction itself requires a give and take, a constant series of transactions between people (Becker 1974). We need to be at least partly in control of this process in order for it to work succesfully in the first place. Not only does personal control give much needed support to the self in terms of boosting confidence, self-esteem and well-being in general (Branden 1985) but it also has the effect of giving shape and direction to our feelings and desires. Thus control is crucial for the care and maintenance of the self in social interaction (Goffman 1959, 1983).

Another reason why control is so essential is that it helps us to reduce the uncertainty and unpredictability of events and people in social life. Trying to be in control, or have some control over how encounters will turn out (say, for or against your interests, smoothly or conflictually, and so on), allows you to have some say in the outcome. Although you can never fully control people or situations (and nor would you necessarily want to), it does help reduce the uncertainty surrounding the outcome. This is a natural tendency since it also allows you to have some input into directing the flow of events rather than being passively 'carried along' by them.

To feel as though you are competent (Franks 1974) and efficacious is also a crucial building block of self-esteem (Branden 1985). Not only does it promote a sense of self-confidence and self-reliance, but it also gives you some leverage in avoiding helplessness or dependence on others. Finally, control or the effort to influence events and outcomes are means by which we get a handle on the future. This is implied by what has already been said about attempting to reduce uncertainty and avoiding excessive dependence, we are thereby able to step into the future with more confidence about what it is we want to achieve and how we're going to make it come about. It makes us *feel* more secure about an inherently uncertain future.

The flexible self

Your 'self' is static or fixed. You're not stuck with it from birth for the rest of your life. You develop as an individual over time. Bits get added, others are left behind as you age, and as you pass through important phases of life. Moreover, the self is many-sided anyway. There's not just one essential you. You have several 'sub' selves or personalities all of which play a part in 'representing' you at different times and circumstances (Goffman 1959, Turner 1988). At key points in your life, different aspects of yourself may come more to the fore (Stebbins 1970); furthermore, you may take on quite new aspects (or even whole self-images). These reflect the scripts, narratives or story lines by which you live (or have lived) your life (Cohen and Taylor 1976, Giddens 1991, Canter 1994). They are self-constructs chosen from a cultural array and shaped by yourself.

Of course, to say that the self is flexible and that it is evolving, changing and 'becoming' (Rogers 1961) in the light of your experiences doesn't mean that you wake up each day with a new self. Although some changes may be fairly abrupt and deliberately designed to make a particular impression, like a fashion make-over, or the adoption of a new lifestyle, most changes in the self are fairly slow paced. They tend to follow the experience of a turning point in life that marks some significant transition.

Reaching certain ages and phases of life development such as childhood, adolescence and adulthood are typically accompanied by substantial changes in body image and self-concept. Also key passages in life such as getting married, or divorced, having children, being promoted, living through a critical illness, and so on, regularly entail alterations or adjustments in the self (Stebbins 1970). This is not simply a reflective intelligence at work here, rationally changing according the stories we wish to tell about ourselves as our lives unfold. Transitions like this also include changes in feelings, values and opinions, and many of these are hard-won in the face of our own entrenched attitudes and emotional commitments. The process of change is often a struggle, a series of disruptive mini-crises rather than a smooth, even, development. Sometimes, the emotional freight we carry around with us, encoded in our memories from childhood to the present, may create an inertial drag that inhibits change. But more importantly, the ballast of feeling that we have acquired through life experiences, always informs and influences the direction of changes in the self.

While we continually monitor ourselves with a view to any revisions we may wish to make, there are also 'core' aspects of the self that remain in place, or are, at least, much slower to change (Turner 1988). These provide an essential thread of continuity, consistency and coherence to our identities and our life narratives. After all, it is rare to find that, overnight, your friend or lover has changed beyond all recognition! Such fundamental changes would be unsettling for others, to say the least, and would tend to destabilize existing relationships.

Such rapid and alarming changes would almost certainly raise questions about your continuing trustability – how do people know whether you are still trustworthy? Can they still count on you? Do they really *know* you any more? Some consistency and continuity of the self is also crucial for underpinning a reliable sense of oneself, of self-knowledge. You need to have a relatively stable sense of who you are in order to buttress your self-confidence, self-reliance, self-esteem and psychological security. A collapse or loss of self, or serious confusion around it, are common features of mental disorder, either results of it or as factors leading up to it.

Much more easily changed, and with less serious consequences, are the more peripheral aspects of the self. I shall refer to these as 'satellite' selves or 'sub-personalities'. As they imply, they are subordinate to the core elements, but nonetheless perform an important role in our lives. We tend to play out these sub-personalities as they are appropriate to different situations and groups of people. An example of this is the way some sportsmen and women are ruthless, aggressive competitors when playing sport, but soft and gentle in their private lives. Another, is that some loving couples seem to change personality when switching from their own 'private' company, to that of friends or acquaintences. Differences in behaviour at work (in front of colleagues) and at home ('in front' of parents, children, or friends) may be quite marked, and carefully segregated so as to reduce any confusion that may arise as Goffman (1959) has pointed out.

Sometimes parts of the self may be shielded from others and in such cases a person may be living a 'secret life' alongside a more public and conventional one. This is the case with some criminals (serial murderers for instance). But secrecy is just as important for unfaithful lovers, spies and con artists. Generally though, segregating audiences to different performances of the self is less dramatic in its implications. Messing up, by inadvertently revealing bits of the self strictly reserved for another audience, is typically met with simple embarrassment or momentary loss of poise.

There is no doubt though, that there is an important distinction between the public and private aspects of self. The inner private world of the individual – what he or she really thinks about themselves and other people, what they've done in the past for which they are ashamed, what indiosyncracies of taste, habits, addictions, fears, insecurities they harbour – is of course, much more 'hidden' from public scrutiny. There is an almost unspoken assumption that there will be, at least, some difference between what a person says and what they actually believe. What people say and do behind the protection of their front doors, and in the company of their nearest and dearest, may be shockingly at odds with their behaviour in public.

Before leaving the issue of the flexible and developing nature of the self it is necessary to flag what will be an important part of my later arguments. This concerns the idea of understanding the self as an 'emergent narrative' rather than a 'revisable' (and by implication, an inherently 'disposable'), storyline. This is important because the idea of a revisable narrative suggests two rather unfortunate and erroneous characteristics of the self. The first is that the self is so prone to change that it becomes almost a ghost, a virtual impression of a human being rather than a real and solid person. This error derives from a lack of distinction between the core and satellite selves (or between the biographical self and situational selves). Those who omit this distinction overstress the revisability of the core aspects of self and underestimate their robustness and durability which derive from the need to maintain consistency and continuity of identity in social interaction.

Second, the idea of a revisable narrative suggests that people have unfettered mastery over their destiny. Since only people can 'revise' anything, the influence of the rather more 'impersonal' circumstances of a person's life are deftly, but strangely, erased from the picture. For example, features such as a person's life chances, living conditions and personal relationships (such as a disabled parent or an unhappy relationship with your partner). Such elements are neither easily revisable nor disposable, but at the same time have a massive (emotional) impact on the self.

In this sense the self is the outcome of the dual influence of volitional decisions on behalf of the person as they buck against the contraints of life circumstances. The self is never freely revisable, it is always conditioned by life events, relationships and social circumstances. Thus the evolution or personal growth of the self is better captured by the notion of an 'emergent narrative' which is able to incorporate this dialectical process.

The higher self

Potentially everyone has access to a spiritual or higher self. However, unlike the other dimensions or properties of the self, some individuals may not develop this spiritual dimension to anything like its full extent. It needs a sensitivity and awareness which some individuals do not possess. However, it is not simply a question of acquiring an ability or skill (which mostly, can be learned anyway). It also depends on a real desire to make a connection with the spiritual side of the self. Some may actively resist, or reject such an idea. Hence it may remain only as an undeveloped potential.

Many academics and sceptics find the idea of a higher self very difficult to accept. Some scientifically minded thinkers feel that accepting such a proposition threatens their rational, materialist world-view. This not really true. Only if their materialist view of the world dogmatically rejects the exploration of non-material phenomena like ideas, values, feelings and transcendental experiences would there be such a possibility. But material and non-material worlds are properly understood as intertwined with each other and not at odds, or in competition. However, some spiritual and new-age thinkers embrace the idea of a higher self, but would reject the view that it has pragmatic links with the social world. They might also object to the idea that control is an essential element of the self, on the grounds that it goes against the essential altruism, care and compassion associated with the higher self. But we must not make the mistake of equating control exclusively with its darker side of exploitation, selfishness and manipulation. This simply overlooks the crucial role of mutual benign control in our everyday lives.

Furthermore, writers on personal development and self-transformation who stress the importance of the higher self have to cease to think of the self as split into two basic components. That is, the ego with its selfish (egotistic) interests on the one hand, and the higher self on the other, with its altruistic, selfless motives and concerns. This model, is far too simple if it is to account for the complexity of the human mind and our involvement in social life. (I discuss at length some of the problems and issues raised by the self-help and spiritual development literature in Chapter 5.)

The organization of the self and types of awareness

Let us move from a consideration of the general dimensions and properties of the self to the internal organization of the person. We must return to some of the issues already discussed (such as emotion, motivation and so on), but view them from a different angle. This involves entering the subjective territory of the person, endeavouring to see the world from their point of view. In Figure 1.2 the left-hand column lists the inner facets of the self which also act as types of awareness – or ways of perceiving and thinking about the world. The right-hand side refers to the organizational and executive parts of the self.

On the general question of awareness I draw mainly on existential philosophy (specifically the work of Heidegger 1962 and Sartre 1966), and humanistic psychology as expressed in the works of Maslow (1968) and Rogers (1961). These writers stressed a view of the human self as largely consciously aware of his or her intentions, plans and purposes. This is directed against the Freudian view that we humans are 'driven' creatures whose thoughts and behaviour are 'determined' by unconscious forces (mainly sexual and aggressive), which are sealed off from conscious awareness.

The idea that the self is, in the main, consciously aware of what the person is up to, is a feature of the existential critique of Freud. Sartre, in

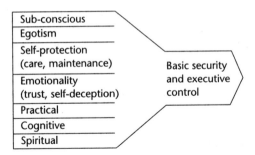

Figure 1.2   Self and types of awareness

particular, is very much opposed to the determinism implied in Freud's notion of the unconscious and I am inclined to agree with him on this. Sartre objects to the notion of an 'unconscious' realm on the grounds that it is difficult, not to say impossible, to understand how something that we cannot reflectively know, or have access to (the unconscious), can determine, or cause our reflective behaviour and thoughts, without us actually being aware at some level that this is what is happening.

It is surely difficult not to agree that normally we are *at least partly aware* of the motivations and reasons for our behaviour, although we may disguise them from ourselves and others, or rationalize them away, or even repress them from full conscious awareness. Sartre's idea of self-deception ('bad faith') and the more general existential notion of 'in-authenticity' seem to offer some purchase on these issues. In short, our behaviour is never fully 'determined' by the arbitrary whim of uncon-scious drives or forces. We are always at least, in part, in touch with our feelings and motivations. However, we are also capable of deceiving our-selves into thinking that we are motivated by unknown 'forces' (wishes, desires) which are completely beyond our control.

The subconscious

It is important to view the self (as Branden suggests) as 'a unifying centre of awareness' – a centre which monitors different *levels and types* of aware-ness. But I must emphasize that this does not rule out the idea of a 'sub-conscious' in which reside the highest levels of repression and the lowest levels of awareness. For instance, traumatic memories (say from child-hood) may indeed be more 'repressed' in this sense or more 'deeply locked away' from conscious awareness, but both these 'operations' imply some level of deliberateness or intentionality on behalf of the 'owner' of the memories. While the radical Freudian view of the 'unconscious' posits the existence of a state of complete human non-awareness and a deterministic view of behaviour, the view of the subconscious developed here implies neither of these.

A person's subconscious is always linked to some level (usually low) or type of awareness (emotional, cognitive, practical and so on). Moreover, this subconscious can never formatively influence a person's behaviour totally independently of their awareness. The difference between the subconscious and other types of awareness is that it is a repository for the most deeply embedded and inaccessible of stored memories and experiences. But in itself the subconscious refers to a level of awareness which may underpin any of the other types. So for example 'emotional awareness' of particular stored thoughts, memories or experiences can be either subconscious or fully conscious (or somewhere in between).

Egocentricity and narcissism

That the different types of awareness may be underpinned by differing degrees of awareness is clearly exemplified by egocentricity. Many of those who are habitually selfish, blinkered and insensitive to others rights, needs and interests seem to be blissfully unaware of the inappropriateness and 'unpopularity' of their behaviour. This is why the self-importance of some egotists sometimes seems to know no bounds. On the other hand, those who are not completely hampered by a lack of 'emotional intelligence' (in this case sensitivity to others feelings, which in turn, requires an ability to empathize) often manage to restrain their over-excesses before others are offended or become resentful.

So although people differ in the extent to which they are 'entrapped' in, or free from, an egocentric mind-set, everyone possesses at least some tendency to place their own interests before other's. There seems to be a 'normal' or 'socially tolerated' level of egotism which others will excuse or dismiss for various reasons (a child or disabled person 'doesn't know better', or a person's arrogance may be exacerbated by drunkeness, or legitimate anger). However beyond this point others will begin to avoid contact with the egotist. Thus, by and large egotism must be constrained in order to gain social acceptance on a consistent basis.

Some writers on personal and spiritual development have claimed that egotism runs rampant in our society because the self is purely an ego, which habitually tries to control or dominate others and has little care and empathy, or sense of social responsibility. Thus, they argue that this ego-self should be supressed (even eliminated altogether), in order for the 'spiritual' or 'higher' self to be allowed to emerge. I have already indicated that the notion of a higher self is important, but to suggest that the self is simply an ego in this sense is a vast simplification especially in the context of the present discussion. Moreover, those who make this claim do not distinguish between egotism and self-protectiveness.

At this juncture, having introduced several aspects of the 'inner' organization of the self, I want to highlight the fact that they are all interlinked. None of them exists alone in splendid isolation. Rather, they are mutually interdependent and constantly leak into, and influence each other. Thus although we may distinguish between them for analytic reasons (and indeed it is essential that we do so), we must not assume that they are 'pure' types 'uncontaminated' as it were, by other levels and types of awareness. Accordingly egotism exists alongside the protective type of self-interest (the focus of the next section) and they both exist in conjunction with emotionality and so on. Each person therefore can be identified by the unique blend or mixture of influences of these different aspects of the self.

Protective self-interest

As I hinted earlier, although egotism is often confused with self-protectiveness, it is essential not to make this mistake. Although there may be an apparent similarity between them as forms of behaviour, in fact they are many miles apart. Self-interest, in this sense, is based on a recognition that the self is fragile and hence potentially vulnerable during the course of day-to-day interaction. Viewed in this light self-interest is centred on inner (subjective) support for the self when it comes under undue stress, or 'caring repair work' when attacked or wounded.

Insecurity around the self can give rise to two kinds of self-protection. First, a person may 'defend' themselves, (either aggressively, or with minimal assertiveness), and if successful, this will have the effect of limiting any further damage and generally stabilizing the situation. Second an individual who senses a threat to their self-esteem or competency may launch a pre-emptive strike in order to ward off trouble before it starts. Anticipating when someone is about to insult you, put you down, or make life difficult can lead to such a pre-emptive attack.

The most effective put-downs are often totally unexpected or seemingly 'out of the blue' precisely because their unpredictability instantly places the 'target' on the back foot. Such 'mishaps' often intrude into the 'rough and tumble' of social banter and in the event the individual must be able to quickly regain social poise and self-confidence otherwise anxieties will build up and affect everyone in the encounter leaving them all feeling awkward and ill-at-ease. But the greatest need for self-protection is perhaps displayed by those who are the least likely to properly defend themselves against threats to their emotional security. That is, those who are already chronically insecure or confused around personal identity, or are habitually defensive and apologetic about themselves and their behaviour. In these people (who incidentally often suffer from mental disorders), vulnerability of personal identity frequently translates itself into avoidance and withdrawal from social life, sometimes even self-imposed isolation. Typically though, at the same time they crave the intimacy and bondedness that is so lacking in their lives.

The altruistic self

In many ways egotism, protective self-interest, and the altruistic side of the self are different facets of the social involvement of the self, or how personal identity divides itself between different ways of relating to others socially. By modulating your egotistic desires you are acknowledging the importance of not alienating others, of not frightening them off, if you are to continue to gain anything in return (to receive back) from your relationships. People will cease to transact with you (over emotional as well as material goods) unless you take their interests and desires into account on a consistent basis.

Likewise the notion of self-protection is a recognition of the vulnerability of self-identity in the flux and chaos of interpersonal encounters. In order to relate successfully to others you must must take 'care' of yourself, keep yourself in good working order so to speak. It is also so with the altruistic side of individuals. We sometimes like to think that altruism derives from an open-ended commitment to compassion, and care of others, of looking out for their interests simply because ethically it is the right thing to do. Usually however, it's not as straightforward as that.

Self-protection, altruism and the restraint of selfishness are three aspects of a similar impulse – to join in with others and have meaningful social relationships with them. Thus they represent the socially involved side of the individual. From the point of view of society and social life they represent moral–ethical rules which underpin the social order of encounters (Goffman 1983, see also Layder 1993 and 1997). Within encounters there is a tendency for those involved to 'look out' for others by deliberately refraining from embarrassing them, by helping them get through, and over, mistakes, gaffes, or otherwise inappropriate responses.

We save face for others and mutually attend to each other's needs in order to create a smooth encounter in which everyone feels OK and obtains something (even if only a feeling of satisfaction) from it. It is important to state that this is only a *general tendency*. There are no guarantees. The existence of these moral rules and the tendency to honour them will not ensure that they will be adhered to. There is nothing to prevent someone who is fiercely determined to insult another, or prevent a fight from breaking out if it must, nor is there anything that that will stop people feeling ill at ease during a formal occasion.

However, the smoothness and orderliness of the majority of encounters depends in large part on general consent to these unspoken rules. Much of this impulse may depend on a natural inclination to be sociable, and our capacity for compassion and sensitivity to the wishes, needs and rights of other people. It may be that we are, indeed, the sort of person who routinely cares about other people and is concerned about their well-being. But these 'inclinations' cannot be divorced from the 'gentle' incremental pressure of expectations about what is socially appropriate in the circumstances.

Everyone realizes that if they wish to be treated in a certain manner, they must make the (enthusiastic) effort to do likewise. In this sense we might recall that reciprocal altruism plays some part in proceedings. People care for each other because they also care about themselves (the potential vulnerability of the self) and would hope that others feel, and do, the same. Altruism therefore is not simply an expression of personality, socialization, parental encouragement, or even 'human nature' – although it may be influenced by all these – it is also generated and stimulated by the (collective) experience of social life.

Higher or spiritual awareness

Someone who is greatly influenced by spiritual matters and who feels them to be an important part of their personal identity will, by virtue of this fact, also have great affinity with the altruistic side of the self. Having argued that altruism is an ethical tendency 'encouraged' by the experience of social life in general, and particularly day-to-day interaction, it may seem unsurprising that there would be some coincidence of interests here. However, even though they may result in much the same sort of behaviour (towards others, in particular) it is also clear that such behaviour is rather differently motivated.

The altruism of the social self derives from participation in the co-operative venture of social life, from the lived experience of getting along with people and the accumulated 'best (ethical) practice' which results from it. Spiritual altruism, on the other hand stems from adherence to an ethics of '*required* practice' in dealing with others which is formalized and documented in spiritual or religious precepts. Now while many such precepts have a rather dogmatic and distinctly sacred character (particularly those of a religious origin), even those that are less emphatic about this, have a distinct otherworldly (non-mundane) slant.

What is not generally recognized is that there is here a coincidence between mundane and otherworldly (or sacred) ethical principles regarding how we treat others in everyday life. It may seem odd when attempting to underline common characteristics, but perhaps the most forceful way of illustrating this is to examine the main differences between these two varieties of altruism. The first concerns the extent of the wider context of such ethical ideas and principles. If your behaviour is informed by compassion and care for others on a mundane basis, then your altruism is fairly narrow in its scope of application (although no less important because of it). This contrasts with altruism informed by spiritual or religious ethics which derive from a much more encompassing context of mythology, theology and so on, and apply to a much wider range of behaviour than everyday encounters. Second, spiritual ethics are often codified, formalized and written down whereas mundane ethics are less precise, more intuitive and subject to local variations in interpretation. They are not usually written down or documented, people seem to automatically know what they are, even if they don't adhere to them. Third, worldly ethics are 'voluntary' in character, they are 'policed' informally with transgressors being dealt with 'locally' through ostracism, gossip, ridicule and so on. Religious and spiritual ethics have a more mandatory quality and those who transgress can be expelled from the community of adherents.

So although there is an overlap between interpersonal ethics and spiritual or higher ethics in the form of the altruistic side of human behaviour and the self, they are different in certain important respects. Thus the sources of the higher self may derive from different areas and in this sense the spiritual or religious sources can be understood as separate but connected over the issue of altruism and the self. In this sense both mundane and non-mundane (otherworldly) sources of altruism are mutually reinforcing – not in competition. Thus the notion of a higher self is an important component of the self (in terms of awareness and behavioural predisposition) and should not be excluded (as it is in the main) from sociological or psychological accounts of the self. By the same token, neither should social life (particularly the world of interpersonal relations) be excluded from an account of the higher self.

Emotional awareness and personal identity

Having already discussed emotionality as a dimension or property of the self, there is little to further add about it as a mode of awareness. Perhaps the most important point here is that emotionality is indeed a mode of awareness. But rather than being associated only with a specific object or a delimited range of attachments it must be understood as having a diffuse and all-emcompassing range of influence. That is, instead of a specific mode or focus of awareness it is more like a feeling tone which infiltrates all aspects of awareness.

Thus both positive emotions like love, trust, happiness, empathic understanding and negative ones like anger, rage, resentment, self-deception may become the focus for particular kinds of feeling tone at different times. As such, human beings are in their nature and social constitution 'emotional' beings. There is no aspect of human awareness or behaviour which escapes the wash of the emotions. Moreover the same considerations apply to the executive, power and control aspects of the self. In this respect emotion and power (and control) are closely tied together as integral components of personal identity and individual behaviour.

Cognitive and practical awareness

These aspects of the self refer to the manner in which we process information about the world and arrange it to form perceptions and understandings which facilitate our navigation around and through this world. While cognitive awareness is often exclusively associated with the capacity for dealing with abstract knowledge, in practice there is a large area of overlap between cognitive and practical awareness. It may be that cognition is also more traditionally linked to linguistic ability, or more precisely, the ability to describe and explain things in language form (colloquially, to 'put things into words'). But this is surely a matter of degree since practical skills, require 'understanding' and depending on their complexity, are also subject to more or less complex descriptions.

It is clear that both cognitive and practical aspects of reasoning are associated with intellectual skills. But as both Gardner (1983) and Goleman (1996) have demonstrated, 'intelligence' cannot be confined to these areas alone. There are many different kinds of human talents including those concerned with understanding other people and being able to recognize and deal with their emotions. If 'intelligence' in general is associated with any one particular 'site' it would be as the unifying organizational and executive centre of self-awareness.

This is just another way of saying that ultimately intelligence is not simply restricted to cognitive and intellectual functions but applies to all modes, types and levels of awareness. Even something as simple and practical as hammering a nail into a piece of wood is not as emotionally neutral as it may appear at first sight. We don't approach such a task in an emotionally neutral manner. How we approach it, in what mood, will depend on a myriad of factors. If it was part of paid employment perhaps we might approach it with professional indifference, or with the annoying feeling that we were generally underpaid. If it was for an elderly neighbour it might engender feelings of satisfaction for doing a favour out of care and compassion for those who are frail or vulnerable. If the nail went in crookedly, and this was the fifth time it had happened in fifteen minutes as you constructed a toy for your child to play with, it might be accompanied by despondency, anger or despair.

The executive self: feelings and capacities

The self then is a unifying, organizing and controlling centre for all the modes, levels and types of awareness we have considered and in relation to its general dimensions and characteristics. There are two main sub-units of organization. One is what I call the 'basic security system' of the self and this provides, as it were, an underlying foundation of self-feeling. In particular it houses what Laing (1969) refers to as 'primary ontological security' or an individual's sense of themselves as a worthy, substantial, embodied person who is firmly grounded in the world.

But overall, a person's basic security system encompasses an even wider set of emotional and existential anchors including self-esteem, self-confidence, feelings of loveability, acceptance, inclusion and so on. In Chapter 2, I describe these as a bundle of (predominantly) emotional needs which underpin self-identity both when the individual is alone and when she or he is in the company of others. As a complex of mutually reinforcing needs, the basic security system also creates the problem of how these needs can be satisfied or realized. In this respect the basic security system operates closely with the executive sub-unit of the self.

A person's need dispositions do not automatically provide for themselves. Thus the self is also required to function as an *agent* whose power is predicated on feelings and capacities grounded in competency, self-efficacy, and hence a degree of control. Knowing what to do and how to do it, as a practical accomplishment, is the job of the self as an agent. If these qualities or capacities are weak or absent then the active basis of the self and its ability to make a difference as far as its own destiny is concerned, will be severely hampered. In this sense the basic security system operates in tandem with the executive capacities of the self. They 'lean on' and buttress each other. If one crumbles, the other tends to crumble with it.

The self then, is a complex of emotional and psychological needs and the organized desires and capacities which enable it to move (or drive) towards some form of healthy functioning or self-actualization (as Maslow calls it). But this process is never fully complete. And although certain needs and their satifaction may originally emerge in the human infant in a certain developmental order, all basic security needs remain in a constant clamour for attention at every moment in a person's life as well as throughout their full lifetime. Desires, of course, fuel the psychological predispositions or state-of-readiness of the person and his or her willingness to seek the realization of their desired objects. They are a natural adjunct of both the pattern of needs themselves and the particular strategems and forms of control and influence which are marshalled to secure them.

Chapter Summary

- There are five important dimensions of the self: It is both part of society yet apart from it; people are emotional as well as cognitive beings; self-identity changes and develops over time; self-control and control over others are essential to social interaction; the self has 'higher' or spiritual potential.
- There are different types and levels of self 'awareness' in relation to: the subconscious, egotism, self-protection, altruism, emotion, spirituality and practicality. These modes of awareness often overlap.
- The unity and stability of the self depends on a properly functioning basic security system and the ability to make things happen (exective capacity). Self-identity unifies an individual's consciousness and their unique set of emotional and psychological needs. It also organizes ways of satisfying these needs through mainly benign-control and influence.

2

Emotional Needs and Desires

Chapter Preview

- The nature of needs and desires: is there a hierarchy?
- Core needs: basic security and self-esteem.
- Satellite or orbital needs.
- What is mental health and what ensures it?

Everyone has needs, wishes, dreams, desires which are closely tied up with feelings and emotions. Together, these are often referred to – much less enticingly – as motivations, need-dispositions, drives and so on. I'll refer to them in the more appealing terms of the opening sentence. Irrespective of what we call them, they all point to the fact that we are naturally active beings who seek to satisfy our clamourous needs in order to have a relatively comfortable existence and a fulfilled life. At least this is what we strive towards, although it almost goes without saying that we're often not as successful as we might wish in this quest for fulfillment.

Typically, once we have satisfied one need, another tends to take its place. In the end, usually we have to settle for some kind of compromise in our level of satisfaction, one we feel we can live with, without too much swallowing of pride or thwarted ambition. In this chapter I explore the idea that the self is especially needy with regard to emotional issues around self-esteem and the stability and security of self-identity. Indeed, our mental health and well-being are sensitive indicators of how well or badly we manage the demands of these emotional needs.

Deficiency and growth needs?

The psychologist Abraham Maslow has drawn attention to what he has called a 'hierarchy' of needs, in which some demand more urgent attention than others. Maslow suggests that the strongest and most basic needs are physiological, such as the needs for food, water and warmth. If these remain unsatisfied then you won't be interested in anything else until they are. If you're hungry, for example, this will override any other needs you have. However, if these basic needs are met then the next strongest will come to the fore. These are safety needs and in this respect we need to feel physically as well as psychologically safe and secure.

Feeling safe and secure we progress to the next stage of need which is for belongingness and love. Here we are concerned with acceptance, trust and affection and our ability to both give and receive them. Once these are satisfied we will turn our attention to the requirement for self-esteem. We need to feel that we are respected by others, as well as ourselves. We need to feel that we are worthy and valuable people who possess a significance which can command the attention of others.

Only when self-esteem needs (and the others) have been fulfilled can we concentrate on what Maslow defines as our highest, but weakest need, that of self-actualization. I'll come back to this in a moment but at its simplest this describes our drive or efforts to become what we are potentially capable of becoming. It is the struggle to realize our full potential as human beings. This is the 'weakest' need in the sense that the other 'lower' needs have priority and press for satisfaction before we can attend to self-actualization. Interestingly, Maslow suggests that the lower, stronger needs are what he terms 'deficiency' motives. The fact that we lack something, like food, security, love, or self-esteem prompts us to try to rectify the deficiency, to fill up the lack. Only the thrust towards self-actualization is regarded as what he calls a 'growth' motive. This is because it is the result of an unfolding of possibilities and potentials rather than a striving to acquire or attain whatever it is we are deficient in, or lack. Unlike Maslow I see no reason to exclude the so-called 'lower' or 'deficiency' needs from issues about growth and the development of potential. The needs or motives of security, love, and self-esteem are not simply things you 'satisfy' once and for all, at particular stages in life. It is surely the case that we all struggle continually with such needs, not only at particular stages, but at every moment of our lives. In that sense, they have a continuous effect on our personal growth and development throughout our lives.

In addition, to view needs as deficiencies gives them a negative slant which is misleading. The way we come to terms with ourselves and our relationships in relation to feelings of security, love and self-esteem can also have positive effects on our growth and development. In this sense needs, desires, wishes and so on, are positive, creative and productive; they cannot and should not be simply defined negatively implying an inner 'lack' in ourselves. A craving to be loved, for example, may lead you to be creative and imaginative in an effort to attract a loving partner. If succesful, your subsequent relationship may prove to be very challenging and productive for both of you in terms of expanding your range of feelings and your understanding of others.

Viewed in this light, all needs (except, perhaps, physiological ones) are associated with both deficiency and growth needs and motivations at one and the same time. Similarly, self-actualization is not simply a 'growth' need it can also be linked to some kind of 'lack' or deficiency. After all, you may come to the opinion that you haven't realized your potential, and that it should be your aim to consciously develop what is lacking in you, such as a greater appreciation of beauty, or more compassion for others. It is misleading to divide needs into deficiency or growth motivations since they are always closely intertwined with each other.

The ongoing needs of the self

I'm not suggesting by any means, that Maslow's ideas have no merit. Clearly they highlight some important characteristics of our needs as human beings. In particular the idea of a hierarchy of needs offers insight into why some people get stuck at certain levels of need and are either unable to progress further, or to deal with their current psychological troubles. I agree wholeheartedly with Maslow that as human beings our inner nature is either neutral or good and that what we think of as 'evil' behaviour often appears to be a (secondary) reaction to frustrations of this inner nature. Thus, for example, much light is shed on the behaviour of some serial murderers by viewing it in terms of frustrated self-esteem needs.

So with regard to viewing the development of the individual from childhood to adulthood and beyond, Maslow's hierarchy has strength and credibility. The idea that unless certain needs are met in a progressive fashion a person may become frustrated and seek satisfaction through crime or deviance is useful and insightful. However, if we think of the many ordinary average people who receive the requisite amount of attention, love, acceptance, approval, and so on, the idea that certain needs are fully met or satisfied at particular stages of life is less convincing.

It is more appropriate to view needs and how we deal with them as an ongoing, never-ceasing process. After all, we never stop needing love, but our life circumstances and psychological requirements may change at different points in our lives. Our loved ones may reject us, leave us, or even die. Other loves may take their place and our own needs and responses may adjust accordingly. We might want someone new to love us in a different way, or maybe our new partner requires us to demonstrate our affection rather more than we are used to. Nothing is static with regard to emotional needs. The same is also true of the way in which relationships change over time, for example, more or less emotional support from either our partners or ourselves may be needed at different times.

Furthermore, people are needy in different ways in different kinds of situation. For example you might need a lot of security and support when you're at work, or doing a particular task such as making a speech in public. However, when you are out with friends, family or even strangers, you may feel much more confident and self-assured. Our needs vary in different situations or when we're doing particular things. Even momentary shifts in encounters may sway the balance of emotional needs. You may suddenly feel insecure when confronted by an unexpected event such as an accident or emergency. Or, you may feel anxious and unconfident before meeting a particular person (say your partner's parents or boss) while having met them you realize there was no need to be anxious.

Emotional needs are never settled or given in a once and for all manner. Your sense of security, confidence and self-esteem all need to be reaffirmed from moment to moment. Of course, I'm not saying that these things change so fluidly that you are completely flattened by all sorts of real or imagined slights or put-downs. This would be very unusual. However, the self is fragile and (depending on your sensitivity), it can be gradually undermined if it has a long run of 'bad' or negative experiences.

Potentially, each and every moment of our lives can provide one of those negative experiences. They can range from a situation were you are alone at home thinking negative thoughts about yourself ('I'm hopeless' I'm not strong enough to cope), through to a work meeting in which someone 'puts you down' in front of others by suggesting you are inefficient. In such cases you may suddenly feel insecure and unsure of your self-worth, although you may 'conceal' it from others. Of course, this doesn't necessarily spell complete disaster, but if you are already feeling vulnerable and unsure, its effects may have more serious implications for your mental health. In essence, the long-term bouyancy of your self-esteem, self-confidence and security depend on continued positive feedback or support in the momentary transactions of life.

Basic security and the self

I've suggested that the most crucial needs of the self – security, love and belongingness, and self-esteem – are everpresent, and ongoing. They represent life-issues which are perpetually important for us as individuals in the modern world. They are also an aspect of our creativity as human beings and are intimately related to our growth and development as individuals. It's not really necessary to ask whether some needs are more important than others. They are all important all the time.

A more crucial question is 'what do we need to ensure our well-being and mental health?' In response to this it is possible to identify some core issues. Without doubt a basic sense of security and self-esteem are essential. They are the scaffold on which we hang the other components that go to make up a healthy self-identity. Without a basic minimum of security and self-esteem, many other human needs such as love, belongingness, acceptance and so on, will find it hard to take root or thrive. In this sense a firm core of security and self-esteem is everything. It's the basis on which you stand or fall as a person.

Sometimes we talk of someone being insecure as if this was a normal and relatively fixed part of their personality. We might even describe ourselves as 'feeling a bit insecure' as when we suddenly feel anxious or have a momentary loss of confidence. These usages generally refer to the milder forms of insecurity experienced in everyday life. But they are closely linked with a more disabling insecurity which can seriously threaten your well-being. This ontological insecurity refers to your connectedness with the world and how in touch you feel with reality. If you cannot feel secure in this manner (I won't use the word 'ontological' all the time), in this basic sense, then you will feel troubled, and unhappy to varying degrees. This is clearer if we focus on those of us who feel basically secure. Typically we feel real, alive and whole (not split or fragmented) and as existing 'inside' our bodies. We have a clear, separate, identity which endures over time. We think of ourselves as being worthy, substantial and genuine.

By contrast insecure people often feel unreal and more dead than alive. This is partly because their sense of identity and independence is uncertain and always 'in question' so that they can never take their personal identity for granted. They feel confused about their identity and may feel 'bad', unworthy and useless. Such a person's whole sense of existence is in question to the extent that they may feel themselves to be an 'empty vessel', or simply a contrived response to what others want them to be.

Individuals who are extremely insecure often suffer from severe mental disorders like schizophrenia (see Laing 1969). However, I want to stress here that we all need a certain level of security so that we continue to have a firm sense of identity. Thus in normal everyday life we experience differing amounts of insecurity most of the time and we tend to block out feelings that we identify as potentially threatening.

Self-esteem and basic security

If basic security is about feeling real, alive, whole and autonomous, then self-esteem is closely linked. Positive self-esteem is about feeling 'competent to live and worthy of happiness' or to feel, 'that I am appropriate to life and to its requirements and challenges'. In contrast, to have poor self-esteem 'is to feel that I am inappropriate to life, that I am ... wrong as a person, wrong in my being' (Branden 1985, p. 5). Thus self-esteem and security (or their lack) refer to very basic feelings which underpin a person's attitude to life and other people, and their personal capacity for happiness. On this basis then, we can say that whatever is threatening to basic security will also be threatening to self-esteem. Importantly, like security, positive self-esteem isn't of the same intensity at all times, it can fluctuate according to circumstances.

In everyday life we are continuously bombarded by all manner of assaults on the self which threaten our security. For example, at work your judgement and competence may be challenged when someone criticizes your behaviour, say in dealing with an argument or in treating a 'difficult' customer. You may be insulted, put down or otherwise treated badly by someone, or you might fail to achieve something, like a promotion or an exam pass. The feelings produced by these situations (like embarrassment, humiliation, hurt and so on), need to be handled almost instantaneously in order to regain composure, security and self-esteem as soon as possible. We do this by employing psychological defences or 'remedial work'.

Psychological defences include 'blocking out' which involves the pretence of trying 'not to notice' if something threatening arises. For example, if you ask your partner 'do you really love me?' and he or she replies curtly, 'oh you know I do' and then quickly changes the subject, it is likely that they will be 'blocking-out' or not acknowledging the emotional force of the question because they find it too (emotionally) difficult to handle. Another kind of defence is 'by-passing' (Scheff 1990). This involves trying to hide or conceal a difficult emotional moment (such as the one just mentioned), by disguising it with diversionary tactics such as changing the conversation, or speaking faster, or throwing the spotlight on to someone else.

'Remedial work' includes 'back-tracking' where a basic mistake or otherwise embarrassing moment is retrieved by conceding ground. For example, admitting that you didn't really know what you were doing, or that you were wrong about something, allows you to carry on without too much loss of composure. Another remedial tactic is 'redefining' what actually happened. As it implies, this requires that the other participants or witnesses are able to agree on the new definitions. Redefining includes claims about what you really meant to say, or that your intentions were misinterpreted.

In these and other ways, potentially undermining feelings of failure, anxiety, worthlessness, insincerity or 'falseness', are 'processed' and reformulated to reduce their potency. Of course, being able to do this depends on having a minimum level of security and self-esteem in the first place. It is also necessary to have some personal control and influence in the situation. You can't have control without security and esteem. At the same time you can't feel secure and positive about yourself unless you are competent and have some effective control of your circumstances.

Self-esteem and basic security therefore provide fundamental anchorage points for qualities and attributes such as self-respect, self-confidence, feelings of worthiness, authenticity, acceptance and belonging. These needs group themselves around this core of security and esteem. Again, however, it is misleading to think of them as somehow derivative or of 'secondary' importance. Rather, both sets of emotional needs are interdependent.

What are these 'other' needs

The array of emotional needs which interlock with security and self-esteem are an immediately recognizable group of feelings and emotions (see Figure 2.1). I'll briefly discuss each in turn. However, at this juncture it is crucial to bear in mind that personal power (benign control and influence) is the key mechanism which brings together self and others in this interdependent relationship.

Love: to love and be loved

Each of us needs to love and be loved, and we express feelings of intimacy with others in different ways. Romantic love is important because it allows a continuous depth of intimacy in a relationship which is often also a sexual one. In terms of depth of intimacy over time it parallels the strong loving bond we experience as a child with our parents or caretakers. Of course not all carer-child relationships are good ones and if a child's experiences are unhappy, more than likely they will have consequences in later life. The child may be psychologically 'wounded' and find difficulty in creating intimate bonds with others.

It is often assumed that romantic, sexual love provides the most intimate and intense expression of a loving relationship. However, there are other kinds of love which provide a high degree of closeness. A parent or carer's love for a child is typically of this kind. Love between friends,

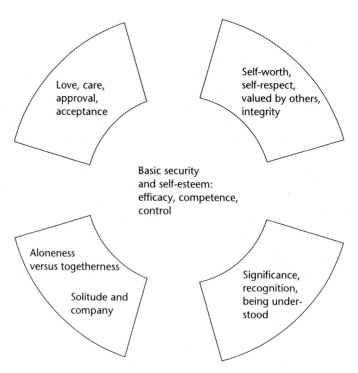

Figure 2.1 Core and satellite needs of the self

neighbours, relatives and so on, are also expressions of emotion, feeling and close bonding. We all need to feel that we are loved in order to feel secure and these relationships are essential to this. The more spiritual expressions of love – say for humankind, or of animals or of the natural environment – are clearly linked to the other kinds of love. However, they are perhaps more essential to an individual's wider personal growth than to the development of basic security and esteem.

Although loving and being loved by others are crucial, the love of self is no less important. All three are interdependent. Without experiencing the love of others it is difficult to have a loving relationship with yourself. Without the love of self the ability to give love to others is hampered. Self-love is not the same as narcissism or an unhealthy preoccupation with oneself – it's not egocentrism gone mad. It's more about accepting who you are and taking responsibility for what you do. It's about having integrity, taking care of yourself and being self-protective when it is required.

The importance of self-love is perhaps clearer if we imagine its opposite, self-hate or self-loathing. This is a condition in which self-esteem is difficult or impossible to generate because you are dissatisfied with who you are. As a result you constantly undermine yourself by having negative thoughts about your abilities, competence and worthiness. Self-hate eats into security and self-esteem like nothing else, leaving you stuck in, or struggling through, quicksand. Happiness and psychological well-being are forever out of reach because there is no basis for having a successful or fulfilling relationship with yourself. Every attempt at enjoyment or feeling good will be thwarted and you will be locked in a frustrated struggle against your very being. Most crucially, perhaps, without self-love, the ability to truly love others becomes a struggle. Thus dependency relationships, or over-bearing, suffocating pseudo-love may take its place, in order to compensate for the absence of true feelings.

Approval of self and others

If love in all its varieties is a key focus for other feelings and emotions, then the need for approval closely mirrors it. Again there are close links between self-approval, approval *by* others and approval *of* others. Approval (in all its guises) is essential for love and loving relationships. Approval implies tolerance (and acceptance) of 'differences' in personality, behaviour and beliefs. This doesn't need to be unconditional or totally 'permissive', but it does require a certain tolerance for other's interests and rights as well as your own.

The search for approval has its own challenges. In the formative period of childhood the child seeks the approval of its caretakers as a means of securing their love. This persists into adulthood where there is a general need for the approval of others, especially loved ones, or those who are admired or looked-up to because they have particular qualities or skills. But this can turn into an unhealthy, excessive need for approval if the individual is uncertain about his or her own independence, rights, responsibilities and effectiveness (the ability to influence things). The constant searching for approval is based on the fear that the other's love will be withdrawn and that you will be left helpless and unloved. This, of course, is an extension of a childhood pattern whereby the individual feels that he or she never received enough (unconditional) approval or love from her or his parents. As a result they learn to feel unworthy and that they don't have the right to expect unconditional love and approval.

Generally it's important to seek the right amount of approval – so that you don't make excessive demands or are rejected too often. Not needing any approval at all, however, is just as unhealthy as seeking too much. It implies a disregard for other's feelings and rights and could lead to tyranny, abuse or domination. Crucially, retaining some independence from other's approval allows you to move away from fear of rejection and to take control of your own decisions and responsibilities.

Self-worth and self-respect

To feel that you have some intrinsic worth as a person and that others value you, as you value them, is crucial for both security and self-esteem. It is difficult to be socially effective if you consider yourself unworthy, or not good enough. Also, having self-respect and thinking of yourself as deserving is an essential condition for happiness. You cannot be happy if you don't think you deserve it. If you feel unworthy or undeserving, you may even sabotage your own chances of happiness. You might even cling to your unhappiness because it has hidden pay-offs, such as gaining sympathy from others, or absolving you from reponsibility for earning a living. An irony of this is that because you are so used to it, you at least know how to get by, or survive within the grip of unhappiness. To even contemplate embracing happiness might arouse great fear and anxiety because it's an unknown and you're uncertain about how to deal with it.

Feeling worthy carries with it the conviction that you feel right about yourself and that you are able to view your actions and beliefs as defensible on moral or ethical grounds. It's not that you constantly go around saying 'what I'm doing is fine and good and therefore I should be valued and respected'. Defensible in this sense means that if challenged, you feel you are on solid ground and that you're OK about explaining your reasons and having them open to scrutiny by others. Your worthiness in this sense, is about creating consistency between your beliefs and actions and recognizing that they express your integrity as a person. A sense of integrity is about feeling whole and unified as a person, rather than uncertain, fractured and full of contradictions and struggles within yourself. Furthermore, if you feel internally harmonized in this way you'll have more self-belief and feel more authentic and genuine. The opposite experience of feeling that you are somehow against yourself, that you never say what you feel, or that you actively mislead others about your feelings and intentions, makes it hard to feel right about yourself. Clearly, not feeling right with yourself can undermine self-worth, self-respect and self-belief.

Being alone and being with others

A tolerance or even a preference for your own company is to some extent a result of being secure in yourself, and of not needing the constant support and approval of others. Seeking periods of solitude away from others, or taking time out from social involvements usually means that you are confident that your own resources are enough for you to feel complete and good about yourself. It indicates that you are to some degree self-reliant and that your feelings of aliveness and intrinsic worth are not entirely dependent on what others think or say about you.

It could be argued that being happy with your own company also means that you are a better partner or companion. This is because being strong and confident in yourself enables you to respect your own and others boundaries and therefore allows you to establish the right balance in relationships. You are not over-dependent on others and are less likely to suffocate or overwhelm them with attention or affection for fear that they might stop loving you, or end the relationship. You are more able to give them their space and freedom to be who they want to be, and this makes it easier for them to do the same for you. We all know, or have had personal experience of relationships where one or both of the partners is/are excessively demanding psychologically and emotionally. Such partnerships lead to co-dependence or addictive love and are based on fear and anxiety rather than trust and genuine love.

Although the wish to be alone is often strong, its intensity varies from person to person. An equally impelling impulse, though, is to seek the company of others and to spend extended periods of time sharing activities. In these periods we exchange information and feelings in both conversational and non-verbal forms (facial expressions, eye contact, gestures, touching, and so on). We need other people to provide us with love, support, approval, bodily contact, reassurance, physical help and a myriad of other practical, physical and emotional needs. In a very basic sense we need others to confirm that we are there, that we exist and that we have an identity that is unique and separate from anyone else. Thus we generally cannot exist for too long without seeking companionship.

Just as an excessive urge to be in company all the time indicates a certain insecurity about yourself, so also the wish for total isolation is an extreme and unhealthy way of life. Again it suggests that some particular fear is directing and driving the individual away from social involvement. The problem seems to centre on some insufficiency or incompleteness of the self. In this case it is the fragility and vulnerability of the self that appears to be the culprit. Unless the self is particularly well-defined and robust in the first place, a person may experience too much contact with others as threatening and anxiety-provoking.

For such a person the normal circumstances of social life – meeting people, going to parties even chatting with friends – can become a severe drain on energy. This is because contact with others is experienced as a battle to keep control over the self and not let it be taken over, stolen or absorbed by others. Life becomes a struggle to preserve the self rather than to assert it by self-presentation in an easy and relaxed manner. Being alone, by contrast, may prove to be much more comfortable because it doesn't require the constant effort to keep the self 'afloat' in the unpredictable and possibly turbulent waters of ordinary life.

Although both trying isolate yourself, or never wanting to be alone are extreme reactions, we all experience a little of each in everyday life. Sometimes we want our own space a bit more than usual, or we may feel the need to get out and be lively, outgoing and sociable rather than stay home and read a book or watch TV. Given that our exact needs will vary, finding a comfortable balance between being alone and being together may sometimes prove to be rather tricky. There is always a risk that our need for space might be interpreted by others as reluctance or rejection. On the other hand, constantly demanding company and entertainment may leave others thinking that you don't respect their need for space. This is a game that we can't win. The need to be separate and the need for involvment are ever-present, and can never be completely resolved.

Significance, recognition and being understood

We all desire to feel that we are 'normal', that we fit in and are accepted by others, that we are one of the crowd. Put another way, we generally avoid being regarded as 'being difficult to deal with' or 'not being part of the crowd'. That is, we don't want to appear odd, strange, stingy or anti-social in any way. It may be true that a few eccentrics might deliberately cultivate personal idiosyncrasies in order to attract attention, but generally their ultimate goal is to be accepted (even if only by a small collection of admirers) and not regarded as complete social outcasts.

However, while the yearning to be accepted and to belong is strong, we strain equally towards being recognized as individuals, and to being thought of as personally significant. Even if in only a minor sense, we wish to stand out from the crowd and not merely blend in with it. We would like our unique contributions to be acknowledged and we want our identities to be honoured as having some special significance in the world. We want to be visible and believed in. We don't want to be overlooked or ignored, as if we weren't there. It's not that we necessarily wish to be famous, or some kind of celebrity (although apparently, many of us wish to be), it's more that we want to avoid *invisibility*. In no matter how small a way, and to no matter how few people, we want to feel just a little bit special.

To feel special is to be recognized as uniquely significant and as a result, to feel we are properly understood. feeling special is the realization that other people have grasped what we are, our essence, our unique being in the world. By contrast, feeling misunderstood is an elemental form of rejection or disapproval which is hard to bear because it cuts deeply into our sense of identity. To *feel* that we are understood (even if we are wrong about this) is crucial, otherwise we may come to think of ourselves as unreachable, unknowable and ultimately, unlovable.

The ever-needy self

In Figure 2.1 the emotional needs of the self have been represented as a sort of cartwheel with a central axis of basic security and self-esteem needs. All the other needs radiate outwards from this while still held within its orbit. These orbital needs both feed into and support this central core, as well as flow from it. They are interdependent with each other and mutually supportive.

It may be true, as Maslow argues, that certain emotional needs emerge in infants in a particular order. However, if the full range has emerged there is no further point in thinking in terms of their relative importance and the potency of their demands for attention. However, of course, at times and for various reasons, not all the child's needs are fully satisfied (say for love) keeping them relatively stuck at a certain level of development. The particular need (in this case for love) will persist as a demanding deficiency in the form of a continuous and overwhelming demand for affection and a sense of belongingness. However, if the full range of needs develops in sequence they will become matted together in such a way that it's almost impossible to think of them separately. They become so entangled that a change in the state of one will have repercussions for all the others. To put this another way, no need or set of needs is ever finally fulfilled or satisfied, all needs constantly demand attention. It may be that the emotional force of a particular need at a particular time, may focus attention on it and seem to drag it away from other needs. But this would only indicate the *relative* intensity of its clamour for attention at that moment in time. Emotional needs are never exhausted or extinguished. They (all) remain continually clamorous for attention.

Thus we can never satisfy our needs and look back on a completed job, so to speak. We are always on the point of trying to balance our accounts. As soon as we come anywhere near to doing so, we are already entrained in dealing with another wave of demands. Everyday life is constantly interrupted

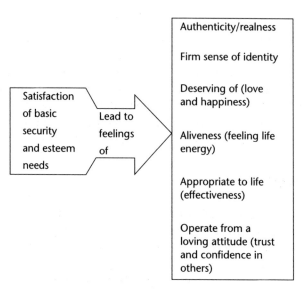

Figure 2.2 The mentally healthy self

by these demands although frequently they are disguised, denied or repressed from full awareness. Moreover, even though we may not be fully aware of them they have consequences – sometimes minor and sometimes momentous – for our conscious feelings, attitudes and behaviour.

What are the consequences for mental health and well-being that follow from this model of the needy self? It is safe to assume that if we can manage the clamourous demands of emotional needs without undue stress and pressure on ourselves, then mental well-being will follow. What then is well-being? If we could see the world from inside the mind of a mentally healthy person what would it be like? What would the constituent elements be? How would we describe the outlook of someone who could be said to be 'in control', well and fully able to deal with life's problems as they arise. I suggest it might be characterized as shown in Figure 2.2.

Essentially, as Figure 2.2 depicts, after developing a fully-functioning basic security system a person would experience the array of feelings listed to the right of the figure. Authenticity is about shedding pretences about yourself. It includes a lack of artifice and being transparently honest and sincere in your relationships (both with yourself and others). To be authentic is to be thoroughly genuine and trustworthy. This, of course, will feed into a firm sense of identity and integrity, because you're not trying to dupe others or trick yourself into thinking that you are something that you're not.

To be inauthentic is to be false to yourself, to be continually playing a role or making an impression in order to manipulate other's feelings and attitudes. The more you have to keep alive various selves or personae for these purposes, the more likely it is that this will undermine the stability of the self and the more unsure you will be about about who you really are. As long as your basic security and self-esteem needs continue to be satisfied then you will feel that you're a deserving human being. That is, you'll feel that it's your right to feel happy, or to receive the love you desire. You won't be plagued by self-doubts about whether you are good or deserving enough to receive the emotional rewards that life may provide. You won't feel too bad about yourself, or so guilty that you're anxious about the possibility of happiness or love. Nor will you sabotage your own chances of happiness because you regard yourself as unworthy and undeserving.

Also you will feel that you are mentally well-balanced and more in touch with life itself. Feeling fully alive endows a person with a vibrancy, an energy and enthusiasm for life and all its possibilities. Perhaps a deeper understanding of this can be gained by thinking of the opposite. For example, of feeling only half-alive or more dead than alive. Or, think of what it might be like to be a spectator of life rather than an active participant, of being a victim, or loser, rather than a doer, an initiator or winner. Those who do not feel fully alive are often defeated by life's problems and are convinced that they remain 'on the outside' of life and excluded from its flow.

An outsider mentality, in this sense, adds up to a feeling of inappropriateness to life, that you're not right for it. It suggests feelings of helplessness and hopelessness as well as the nagging feeling that you can't make a difference to your life. However, if your basic emotional needs are being met in a more or less satifactory manner, the opposite will be the case. You'll feel good about yourself and your worth as a person. You will take pride in you're ability to engage effectively with life, its problems as well as its rewards. You will feel fired-up by challenges and be convinced that nothing will stop you from having your say, of making a difference or overcoming adversity.

The element which adds a final touch, as it were, to the psychological outlook of the healthy person stems from a release from emotional inhibition and self-defensiveness. People whose needs have been frustrated in some way cannot open themselves to the rewards that flow from giving (as well as receiving), in their relationships. People who are thus afflicted operate from a fundamental basis of fear, anxiety and a generally non-trusting response to others. The definition, therefore, of a mentally healthy person is one who operates on the basis of loving, trusting relationships and responds without anxiety both to the 'rewards' and disappointments of life.

The mentally healthy person

Of course this is a model, an ideal of a person in full mental balance. In reality we are all less than perfect. We all have our faults, failings and annoying habits. We are not saints, and were never meant to be. But neither are we wild beasts or evil demons disguised in civilized clothing. Although there are undoubtedly some individuals who could be described as evil (serial murderers being a prime example), most of us fall somewhere in the middle range of ethical behaviour. In this sense we would find it difficult, if not impossible to even contemplate (let alone commit) murder or rape, or engage in torture or bodily mutilation. Not exactly, saints or sinners then, but flawed, albeit in a minor way.

At heart we may well be well-motivated and/or have the best of intentions, but we always manage to fall short of these ideals in some way. This may be because we are occasionally tempted to put our own interests before others, or because we often (unintentionally) misjudge what is 'good' for, or in the interests of others. Put bluntly, sometimes our efforts to do good are simply ill-judged or mistaken.

The average person doesn't have all their emotional needs fulfilled at any one point in time and therefore their attitudes and behaviour reflect this flawed or imperfect character. We all have personal limits and levels of 'guardedness' about ourselves, our weaknesses and our vulnerabilities. We also have different levels of tolerance for other people and their often-times, ill-mannered or unprincipled behaviour. These traits are sometimes regarded as weaknesses, but they are also a natural part of our make-up as human beings.

It is also true that certain so-called character defects, or deficiencies in social skills, reflect the reaction of a 'wounded self' rather than a hatred of others, or a wilful attempt to do them harm. Thus the mentally balanced individual has to be understood against this backdrop of 'imperfection' in temperament and disposition towards others, as well as in relation to ourselves.

I have tried to outline a general model of the different elements that constitute an ideally balanced, or healthy individual. A person's uniqueness resides in their specific profile of need deficiencies and satisfactions.

In this respect we all differ in the nature of our 'flawedness' as individuals. Some of us seem perpetually entangled in issues about approval, or love, or acceptance. Others have more problems, sensitivities and vulnerabilities in areas of self-worth, assertiveness, effectiveness, and so on. Nevertheless, all these areas continue to be of great importance for us all in our everyday lives. They define the points at which we strive to be the person we are and would wish to be.

Chapter Summary

- Deficiency and growth needs are not separate, they are different but essential aspects of all needs and desires.
- All needs clamour for attention continuously and simultaneously.
- There are core needs and satellite (or orbital) needs which arise from, as well as mutually support each other.
- Security and self-esteem needs are core, while love, approval, self-worth, self-respect, significance, acceptance, belonging and recognition are orbital.
- Good mental health or adjustment leads to love, trust, happiness, as well as feelings of aliveness and appropriateness to life.
- We all differ in the nature of our flawedness as human beings.

3

Your Controlling Heart

Chapter Preview

- The nature of desire and its link with self-control and interpersonal control.
- The importance of benign control for the satisfaction of desire and emotional and psychological needs.
- Emotional intelligence and self-control. Avoiding helplessness through positivity and making a difference.
- Dealing with uncertainty and unpredictability.

At first sight it may be difficult to accept you are esentially a creature of control. But be reassured that this doesn't mean you are any less capable of care or compassion. In fact, the opposite is the case. Qualities like care and compassion actually depend on being able to control and influence others! To understand this properly we have to revise what we traditionally mean by control (and power). We must set aside the conventional view of control (and power) as entirely negative and repressive. This view ignores the fact that, in everyday life, benign control is the most widespread and is much more positive and creative. 'Benign' control contrasts markedly with malign or exploitative forms and although both types are related, it is benign control which most commonly figures in our daily life. To understand its role in our lives we must grasp why it is essential to our existence as social beings.

Desire and the need for control

Human desire is at the root of the controlling impulse. As a dynamic force or energy that both propels and orients us to the world, desire compels us to seek its objects. In short, and simply put, we have wants and needs that seek satisfaction. Here, I'm not just thinking of material and bodily needs, like food, shelter, protection and the like, but also emotional or feeling requirements such as intimate bonds (with friends, kin, and romantic partners). Desire spreads beyond the satisfaction of basic human needs that we all require (such as a minimum amount of food or love or companionship).

We are also unique individuals with very specific and sophisticated needs and desires tailored to our individual personalities and life experiences. Some of us need more love and support than others – perhaps because we were relatively deprived of them as children, or because we don't believe we are lovable or deserving of love. Other individuals demand constant ego-grooming in order to confirm their own inflated sense of importance. Yet others need 'to win' at everything they take on, be it a conversation, a game of chess, a pub quiz, or a love affair, in order to alleviate a basic insecurity about themselves and their 'worth' as individuals.

In short, every individual has a unique configuration of desires, wants and needs that demand attention through social contact. Managing or satisfying these sorts of desires/wants/needs is the regular stuff of routine social interaction. We are social, not isolated individuals who have inter-dependent bonds with other people (and institutions). We could not completely satisfy our own needs, even if we were concerned to make the effort. We might try to convince ourselves that we are lovable, but until we experience regular loving relationships, we cannot know this for sure. The fulfilment of desire, therefore, is located in, and dependent on, the social arena of its actualization.

Thus the main way in which we deal with desire is through our daily encounters with others. Every time we enter into the presence of one or more people, we begin the essential and ceaseless job of attempting to present our desires, so that others will recognize them and willingly or (unintentionally) be drawn into the drama of their fulfilment. I say attempting because there is nothing assured or guaranteed about this. We may fail disastrously to gain the attention and respect that we need (and maybe think others owe us) despite our best efforts. The task is fraught with uncertainty and depends very much in our social skills in managing others, as well as on their willingness to accept or rebuff our overtures.

However, despite any rejections we may suffer we can only satisfy our desires through social interaction. We must co-operate, and 'deal' with others and this requires the effective use of people-management skills and self-presentation skills. The two are interdependent. Unless, we come across in a non-threatening manner, as likeable and trustworthy, we are unlikely to bring out the good-will and co-operation of others. Therefore, the most crucial of our social skills concern the use of personal knowledge of others and to subtly, and benignly, 'manipulate' them in order to get what we want, or create a desired state of affairs.

Frustrated desire

If we are unable to master these skills, or for some reason never had the chance to learn them, then we may experience difficulties dealing with others. We may not feel 'at home' with people and hence feel out-of-joint with our social lives. A failure to obtain emotional and material desires may lead a person to feel estranged or isolated from others. In turn, this may push them to express themselves in unusual ways which others think of as strange or bizarre. Such behaviour (say as in paranoia), is regarded as anti-social because it is out-of-synch with 'normal' or conventional behaviour. Even more seriously – in terms of its anti-social consequences – if someone is unable to get what they want through benign control, they may be tempted to use illegitimate means such as crime, force, coercion or exploitation.

Although obtaining our desires depends on the skilled and effective use of benign control, the nature of our desires is also a crucial, and sometimes overriding, factor. You're more likely to obtain your heart's desire if that desire is regarded as normal or socially acceptable and if its object is readily accessible. For example, the wish to find a compatible sexual partner and to live a settled existence with them would receive strong social support, regardless of whether you are any good at finding or attracting a potential partner.

However, to use an extreme example, if you harbour urges to have sex with dead bodies, or to sleep with dismembered body parts (as did the notorious serial killers Jeffrey Dahmer and Dennis Nilson) then you will, thankfully, be severely hampered by the forbidden, not to say illegal, nature of your desires. The social acceptability of your desires has an important bearing on the way in which you can attempt to satisfy them. Forbidden desires, more than likely, require the use of illicit means such as deception, force, exploitation and so on.

The range of desire

It is important to think of desire not only as concerned with sexual matters, but as *anything* to do with an individual's personal wants and needs. Forbidden desires may thus be directed at material objects like drugs or stolen property as much as about deviant or 'perverted' sexual preferences. Similarly, acceptable desires may include the quest for spiritual fulfilment, or the wish to do good deeds, as much as it may centre on the acquisition of sports cars, designer clothes or expensive restaurants.

Further, desire should not only be thought of as a defensive or automatic response to a lack, or deficiency in ourselves, such as lack of love or personal significance. Although such feelings may initially set desires in train, their actual pursuit may give rise to creative and productive behaviour. If you desire to be a more popular person, you will need to break out of old habits and adopt new ones. You may have to find new, or original solutions to old problems about how to get on with others or, how to present yourself more effectively. This applies equally to the pursuit of forbidden desires, regardless of their consequences and moral implications. Thus it is, that serial killers may be highly 'creative' in selecting and entrapping their victims, as well as in the concealment of their crimes or in blending in with their surrounding communities. Creativity is not limited to ethically sound desires – it may be in the service of good or evil. In this sense, the elements of control (benign or malign), involved in the attempt to fulfil desire, must also be understood as essential to this creative enterprise.

The controlling self

Desire, emotion, feelings, wants and needs then, are major impulses which give shape and direction to human behaviour. But these impulses presuppose a self who does the controlling in order to achieve these things. Thus emotional energies flow around the self giving rise to behaviour which in turn feeds back into our self image. In this sense the self can be a many-faceted thing. Over the lifespan our self-identity is shaped and reshaped according to altered circumstances and critical experiences such as marriage, parenthood, illness, getting older.

Also, in general terms, our self-identities are fairly flexible although not entirely fluid. Generally it is wishful thinking to view ourselves in a static, simplified manner – say as a 'together', blissfully happy, selfless person who always behaves 'sensibly', or logically. No matter how 'in charge' of ourselves we may appear to be, there are always times when this mask cracks or slips and we reveal some of our more (so-called) 'irrational' impulses. There are times when, despite our best efforts to put on a happy face, we actually feel 'down', lonely or sad. Sometimes, this may be simply a fleeting mood that quickly disappears, at others it may signal a prolonged period of depression.

I'm not denying that there are some people who seem to be always on top of things, in touch with themselves, and unfazed by the problems of life. It's also true that some individuals appear to be constantly troubled, oppressed, helpless, and pessimistic. Clearly, these are recognizable types of people. But given the right circumstances, each of us is capable of experiencing an array of feelings. We are never simply trapped at one point on the spectrum. Our emotions are a muddy mixture of harmonious and conflicting influences. A seemingly happy, untroubled and care-free person may be putting on a front to disguise real feelings and desires. On the other hand, the saddest person may occasionally see the more ironic or humourous aspects of life. In sum the self may be a place of calm fulfilment or of troubled woundedness.

Self-control

In children, a lack of self-control is usually tolerated because they have not yet learned or acquired the skills needed. However, adults who display a lack of self-control are typically regarded with suspicion or mistrust. They pose a threat to the conventions and rules that normally guide our relations with others. In this sense self-control implies suppressing your underlying feelings (and any behaviour that expresses them), so that you don't embarrass yourself or other people, or put you, or them, in 'difficult' and avoidable situations. So, for example when you've been invited round for dinner at your spouse's parents or boss, you don't say 'My God I'm starving!', as soon as you get through the door! Or, when you're in the middle of lovemaking, you shouldn't start talking about what sort of day you had at work, or the latest sports results – even if you are indeed preoccupied by such thoughts.

On the surface self-control appears to be the result of a purely private, inner process and there are some examples to reinforce this view. For instance, controlling what you eat (dieting) or how much alcohol you drink, or making a determined effort to be more polite to others all suggest that self-control is about an internal process of self-mastery, of being in charge of yourself. However, if we scrutinze these more closely, and as the previous examples make clear, self-control is also closely linked to social life in a number of ways. There are social pressures on us to learn the skills of impulse control because we soon realize that our social acceptability is dependent on it. Too much inappropriate behaviour will get you a bad reputation and people may start avoiding you. In the long-run, this will drain you of your power (of attraction) over them. So your lack of self-control will lead to diminishing control over others. Anticipating this is one reason why we tend to bow to the social 'rules' about impulse control in the first place. Similarly, controlling your weight, alcohol consumption, or manners may be ways in which you attempt to boost your attractiveness (and hence power), over others. Alternatively, forms of eating disorder such as anorexia of bulimia may be an attempt to obtain some personal control where it is otherwise absent or difficult to retain (Rowe 1988). Thus control over the self is tightly linked to control over others, while controlling others always has implications for the self.

Emotional intelligence

The role of emotion in our personal lives underlines the interconnection between self-control and control over others. Goleman (1996) has examined how 'social' and 'emotional intelligence' play an important role in shaping how well people cope with the practicalities of life. The ability to understand others and act wisely in human relations are essential to many aspects of self-control. For example, people who are able to recognize and monitor their feelings as they happen have greater certainty about the the direction of their lives and the crucial decisions they make say, about marriage partners or what jobs to take. Likewise, if you can handle or manage your feelings you are more likely to be able to bounce back from life's setbacks and shake off anxiety and negative attitudes.

Emotional self-control or the ability to delay gratification (and hence stifle impulsiveness), is crucial to achieving success in life. It encourages you to be self-motivated and effective in whatever you do. Likewise, empathy – the ability to recognize and understand other's feelings is an essential people skill. It is associated with caring, compassion and altruism (and is notably lacking in violent offenders like rapists and serial killers). Similarly, emotional intelligence is linked to the ability to handle relationships by managing emotion in others. People who are particularly adept at this have high social competence, are popular and make good leaders. They are very effective in interpersonal skills (Goleman 1996, pp. 42–3).

It is clear that what Goleman (and the other authors he draws on) identifies as key components of emotional intelligence are exactly the sorts of things I have highlighted in relation to self-control. Being able to control one's temper, to hold back inappropriate expressions of emotion, to control impulsiveness and so on, all involve emotional intelligence in the pursuit of self-composure and the social rewards it brings. People skills, handling relationships, managing other's emotions and interpersonal effectiveness are all bound up with issues of control of the self and others.

Although self-control, or 'being in control' may refer to a diverse range of things from suppressing your own anger, or being able to pacify someone else, to subtly manipulating others by showing that you recognize and respect their feelings, they all highlight the connection between self and other control. Clearly, self-esteem, self-belief and self-confidence allow you to feel able to cope with difficult situations and to deal with your own and other's emotions. In short it invests you with a sense of mastery, a feeling of effectiveness over your own life as well as over those whose behaviour affects you.

Avoiding helplessness and making a difference

Drawing attention to the fact that self-control is always, in some way, connected to social life and other people's behaviour, underlines the social nature of human agency – in other words – human being and doing. As I've intimated already, this doesn't mean that the individual has no 'private' or personal areas of his or her own. Such 'spaces' are partly freed from social pressures, expectations and constraints in which you can preserve some feeling of uniqueness and distinctiveness from others. But this privacy must always be understood *in relation to* the social circumstances and relationships which make up your life. Your private life is never completely separate from social life, just as the social world is never completely free of the influence of individuals.

In this sense we are desiring beings who are concerned to make an impact on our lives and the world we inhabit. As social beings, we (naturally) have the will, and seek the power to influence others. This is what recognizing and handling our own, and other's emotions is about. It is the attempt to control – the practical application of our human powers. Again, though, we must not be misled into thinking of power and control simply as negative, prohibitive and restrictive. Benign control releases energies directed more towards the positive, expansive and liberating to varying degrees of course. Not everyone is selflessly motivated, all of the time. Even the most altruistic of us is, to some extent, caught within the net of egotistic desire.

Part of the urge to control is centred on the mastery of, and ability to transform, our circumstances. We don't like to think that we are 'trapped' say, in a marriage or partnership that isn't working, or that there is no way out, or of making our lives better, more comfortable or more fulfilling. Of course, it's not always possible to overcome some circumstances. If you've got an illness like cancer which has progressed to a terminal stage, then it is inappropriate to talk of 'transforming' such an unfortunate situation entirely. However, depending on your resilience, fortitude and sheer will to stay alive, it may be possible to prolong your life, or at least make the time left more fulfilling in some way.

Much the same goes for those trapped in poverty or dead-end jobs. It is always possible, given the required motivation and initiative, to adapt to limited opportunities so as to stave off a victim mentality and make the situation work for you. In these instances it's more a matter of making a bad situation more tolerable than a wholesale change-around in fortune. Clearly also, some people find it more comfortable to 'embrace' and remain in circumstances which, for others, would be intolerable. For example, there are often hidden psychological pay-offs for remaining in a victim status. There are people who prefer to be always ill because of the attention it attracts, rather than to actively try to recover and change their situation.

In a case such as this it would appear that the person gives up on taking responsibility for their lives. However, in another sense it could be interpreted as their way of getting by, of making a seemingly dead situation work in their favour. In that particular sense it is all about control over one's circumstances, albeit in a rather negative manner. Apart from these, there are sometimes other very compelling reasons for remaining in bad situations. For instance, people often become entrapped in dead-end jobs because of family commitments, or because they would miss out on welfare or pension benefits should they try to move to better jobs.

Positivity and the self

Overall though our natural tendency is to move away from situations in which we feel helpless and to try to obtain at least some control of our circumstances by modifying them whenever possible. This draws our attention to a deeply-valued psychological characteristic of human beings. That is a general attitude of positivity towards life, a tendency to go forward and not give up on ideals, or give in to problems and bad luck. Such an attitude speaks to the will to live, to embrace life and to face it with optimism and fortitude despite the inevitable problems and disappointments we encounter. We respect and honour this trait in other people as well as ourselves since it is affirmative of life rather than defeatist.

But the whole idea of a positive attitude towards changing our circumstances depends on our acceptance of self-responsibility. We can only confidently embark on making our lives better, if we believe that we, ourselves, are capable of initiating and carrying through changes. To be dependent on others, in this respect is either to be a victim or an underdog who relies on the goodwill or benificence of others. Of course, there are those who are genuinely vulnerable or helpless and in need of protection. But generally speaking, it is always in your own interests to have some control over your life, to have some independence from others.

Thus the ability to alter the circumstances of your life is dependent on your belief that ultimately, you and you alone, can make things happen. It is only you who can enhance the quality of your life, by changing habits or attitudes, or acquiring new skills, indulging in fresh experiences and forging social links and bonds with an increasing circle of friends and acquaintants. It almost goes without saying that the capacity to energize and motivate yourself in this respect requires a minimun level of self-confidence, self-esteem and self-reliance.

It also has to be appreciated that the project of achieving a more dynamic and effective self is intimately tied up with your feelings and emotions. The more self-reliant and in control of your destiny you become, will alter and shape how you feel about yourself and others. Expanding self-awareness and self-confidence will produce new levels of emotional experience and qualitatively change the nature of your involvements with others.

Unpredictability in social encounters

This leads us to examine the very nature of social interaction itself and how it is linked to personal control. I want to highlight the importance of what could be termed the persistent problems that we face each time we come into contact with others and have meaningful exchanges with them. The three problems are uncertainty, unpredictability and dealing with the future and, as may be apparent, they are all closely related.

The problem of unpredictability centres on the fact that we are all unique individuals with different attitudes, opinions, experiences, emotional needs, moods, feelings and so on. When we interact with each other we bring these different characteristics into play. However, successful interaction depends on the participant's abilities to take each other's attitudes and predisposi-tions into account so that areas of ageement or disagreement are clearly marked out. So even if we agree to disagree with someone we always know where we stand with them. Mainly we try to gain some level of agreement and rapport with others (even if we don't much like them), because we want to get 'something positive' out of the transaction.

This may be a piece of information such as how to find a particular street or neighbourhood, or it may be permission from your boss or your parents to take time off school or work. It might be that you are simply looking for emotional reassurance from the person you're talking to. Of course, the actual subject and substance of transactions are immensely varied. However, even if it goes wrong in some way, say for example, an argument ensues, or you both feel emotionally troubled, you want to understand what has happened and why. To achieve this mutual understanding (not necessarily, mutual agreement), everyone involved has, to some extent, to overcome their differences, preferences and prejudices so that communication is based on shared assumptions.

Also, each person has to try to see the other person's point of view, to put themselves into the other's position, to get into their shoes, to see where they're coming from (even if they don't agree). Without these common points of reference the encounter will be chaotic, confusing and unfulfilling. At the same time as trying to see where the other(s) are coming from, we are attempting to predict how they will respond to us. We try to anticipate what they will do, or how they will react, so that we can line up our next response or conversational gambit. We attempt to predict how others will react in order to keep the encounter on a stable footing, so that we can get something out of the experience.

However, prediction is always imprecise and, therefore, provisional. Because we are all products of unique patterns of experience, other people's responses are inherently unpredictable. Even if we think we know somebody 'inside out', they are always capable of surprising us and responding out of character. They may be the kind of person who is *always* changing their minds about certain issues and hence this adds a further complication. Furthermore, encounters themselves are difficult to predict accurately. The agenda is constantly unfolding, people switch positions according to how things are going, what 'alliances' are forming and what the collective mood and atmosphere is like.

Dealing with uncertainty

Because of the unpredictability of people and encounters, there is always some uncertainty about the outcome of social interaction. We have no real idea whether a meeting will turn out to be smooth and 'uneventful', or whether a particular person will react the way we want them to. However, if we were to approach each encounter from the point of view that it was all going to be a big mess, totally chaotic and hopelessly confusing, we would never summon up the courage to communicate with anyone. Thus we tend to approach encounters *as if* we could predict the outcome and how people will react. We start from fairly sketchy, but coherent expectations of how things will go. Once we are 'in', and the encounter gets started, these prior assumptions get modified and reshaped as the interaction takes on a small life of its own.

In this sense an orientation to control makes us feel comfortable and 'in-synch' with the other participants. It allows us to go through with the encounter with composure and some confidence that we will gain something from it – even if this is 'only' a pleasant feeling of inner satisfaction. This is perhaps easier to envision if we imagine the opposite of this. If we feel awkward, out-of-kilter and that we, or the experience itself, is getting uncomfortably out of control we will try to get away from the situation.

If we are more in tune, comfortable and in touch with things and feel that we have *some* control, the more likely we are to remain and enjoy the experience. We may even try to prolong the encounter because it has become pleasurable and satisfying. This is commonly seen when people stay on the telephone to talk about nothing in particular, or are reluctant to break off a meeting, simply to extend or deepen the bonding that the conversation provides (Tannen 1987, 1992). This is most frequently the case between those who have already established intimate bonds such as lovers, friends or family members. Nevertheless it is not unknown to occur between people who have just met.

To put this in slightly more formal terms we could say that we approach encounters with 'an orientation to control' which we have learned from accumulated experience. Previous encounters have made us aware that unless we adopt this stance, the encounter may provide us with some-thing less than a smooth ride. The more stability we can inject into the encounter, the more satisfying will be the outcome. Of course, we can never achieve full control, there will always be uncertainties and risks to be taken. In fact, their existence is partly responsible for generating excite-ment and euphoria in many encounters.

The point of the control orientation is to *try* to minimize risk and uncertainty to the point where we feel confident that we can deal with them. We must view them as, at least *potentially* manageable, otherwise we will shy away from the encounter in the first place, or if it is already underway we'll attempt to leave at the earliest opportunity. The tendency to seek a minimum level of control is a kind of safeguard against poten-tial pitfalls – like heated arguments, embarrassment, or humiliation. By carrying through with this orientation throughout the encounter we are able to meet problems as they arise, and thereby keep us on an 'even keel'.

Of course, although it's a safeguard, it's never an absolute guarantee that things will go swimmingly well. Despite everyone's best intentions, encounters can get out of control, as when seemingly peaceful gatherings or conversations suddenly erupt into anger, disarray, confusion or even violence. But the control orientation not only 'prepares' us for interac-tion. Social life is a fast moving blur at the best of times, and once the encounter is in train, the orientation to control allows us to stay in touch with events as they swiftly unfold. At the same time it enables us to have some say in shaping the outcome.

It is the uncertainty of the future outcome and the riskiness entailed in its unfolding that is the important issue. We try to anticipate and manage the unknown future by assuming that it is somehow controllable. But we are well aware of the 'tragic' nature of our efforts. We are compelled to try to bring it within our grasp while simultaneously knowing full well that we can be, at best only partially successful. Despite this discomforting realization we cannot leave ourselves totally at the mercy of fate. Importantly, the control orientation is a way of convincing ourselves that we *can* reduce the uncertainty of encounters and the inherent riskiness of social life.

Chapter Summary

- Desire is creative and productive, it's not simply the result of a lack or deficiency. Desire refers to socially legitimate (or acceptable) behaviour as well as deviant or unacceptable forms.
- Benign control is the means through which we influence others (and they influence us) and hence achieve some degree of emotional satisfaction or fulfilment.
- Benign control includes emotional intelligence which allows us to be sensitively aware of our own and other's emotions, moods, feelings and desires. Being able to control impulsiveness is crucial for behaviour that is socially appropriate.
- A prior orientation to (benign) control enables us to deal with uncertainty and unpredictability in interaction and guards against arguments, embarrassment and humiliation.

4

Desire, Influence and Control

Chapter Preview

- Three types of interpersonal control: how benign control compares with the 'stolen' and 'exploitative' types.
- The varieties of benign control and the interpersonal strategies associated with them.
- The ways in which we attempt to satisfy our emotional and psychological needs as expressions of self-identity.

In Chapter 3 I suggested that to be a balanced, mentally healthy person certain emotional needs must be attended to and satisfied. One of these was the feeling of being in control or having some control over yourself, your personal relationships and your life as it unfolds. If you feel that things are 'out of control' or that you don't have any control in certain relationships, for example, with your partner or your boss, then you won't feel so good. You may even become physically or mentally unwell!

In this chapter I consider the variety of ways in which we put our controlling skills into practice to satisfy our emotional needs. 'Benign' control is very important in this regard and helps us deal with our feelings and the emotional needs we require from others. This chapter will again concentrate mainly on the way benign control figures in our everyday emotional lives. To do this, first let me briefly consider it alongside other kinds of control (see Figure 4.1).

Styles of control

Control is most often thought of as something negative or bad, but this only applies to 'exploitative' control and stolen control (Figure 4.1). Benign control, however, is a positive force that works in the best interests of everyone involved. The aim of the benign style of control is to obtain only a partial hold over someone in order to 'guide' them into willing compliance.

Benign	Stolen	Exploitative
Partial	Complete	Complete
Open	Closed	Closed
Mutual (interests)	One-sided (interests)	One-sided (interests)
Appeals and inducements	Appeals and threats	Threats and coercion

Figure 4.1   Three styles of interpersonal control

This is unlike exploitative control in which the controller aims to have as complete a grip on his or her victim as possible, irrespective of their wishes. Benign control is generally a matter of taking each other's interests into account and then coming to some sort of balanced compromise or agreement. It allows each person to gain something satisfactory from the relationship. Each person must feel that they have *enough* control to influence what happens and the way decisions are made in the relationship.

For example, lovers who respect each other's needs and interests generally don't want to completely dominate their partners. Usually they will give them freedom and space for themselves and their personal growth. They communicate openly with each other in order to assess what each needs and how they can be fulfilled. They have a mutual interest of love for each other and therefore, are both concerned with making the relationship work. They 'control' each other in a mutual and benign way by making personal appeals – treating each other as uniquely important and special (see Bernstein 1973). In addition they offer each other emotional gifts and offerings meant to express their mutual love.

If mutual freedom within the relationship starts to deteriorate, then so will its health. If the decay remains unchecked, the relationship may fall apart altogether. The control loses its benign qualities and becomes either 'stolen' or 'exploitative'. Stolen control, as the phrase implies, is about trying to psychologically manipulate another without them realizing it. The controller acts out of purely selfish reasons and aims to make the 'target' completely dependent on them. Communication is one-way, in that the controller keeps back information but deceives the target into thinking everything is out in the open and sincere. Emotional blackmail is a good example of stolen control. Emotional blackmailers use personal appeals or threats in order to get their victims to comply with their wishes. Typically they threaten to withdraw love or support if their victim (very often a family member, a colleague or a friend), doesn't toe the line. By targeting the personal weaknesses or vulnerabilities of the victim, the blackmailer creates in them feelings of guilt and fear. Manipulative ploys like 'how could you treat me this way', 'how can you be so selfish' or 'after all I've done for you', work for exactly these reasons. Personal appeals are mixed in with veiled threats about what will happen if they don't get their way.

Emotional manipulation like this can shade into more abusive control and exploitation. For example, a husband who psychologically terrorizes his wife may also use the threat or actual use of physical violence to reinforce domination. Women abuse is a clear example of exploitative control in which the man wants to keep his partner completely 'under his thumb'. He typically keeps her under constant scrutiny so as to limit her independence or freedom. Threats of violence along with periodic 'doses' of actual physical violence are the punishments meted out to keep the woman strictly under his control.

In the case of women abuse it is also clear that different kinds of control, or different aspects of them, may be used in conjunction with each other. For instance abusive men often have a reputation for being 'charming' in the eyes of those outside the relationship and this helps to conceal the abuse (Horley 2000). But the abuser also finds it useful to employ his charming persona on his victim as well, so that she never knows what to expect. This keeps her under continuous fear and anxiety and she becomes preoccupied with trying to read his behaviour and calm him before he explodes into violence. In short, she becomes preoccupied with survival rather than the possibility of escape.

Varieties of benign control

In the light of this brief comparison we can see that in its ideal healthy form, benign control is very different from 'stolen' or 'exploitative' control. It is also true that the styles of control may be used in conjunction with each other. The possibilities are many and complex. However, here I simply want to concentrate on the way in which we use benign control in our everyday behaviour and relationships as a means of satisfying our basic emotional needs. There are many ways in which we do this but I shall discuss them in terms of four general styles of benign control. These are:

1 Attractors
2 Seduction
3 Striking bargains
4 People skills

Attractors

This style of benign control depends on your ability to attract the kind of attention you require in order to have your basic emotional and psychological needs met. Your attraction may be based on a variety of things, not just physical attributes. Nevertheless, there are physical attributes which can obviously play a role. For example, physical beauty in both men and women can be a major advantage in attracting a romantic or sexual partner in the first place. Physical attractiveness may not be sufficient in itself to hold two people together who have few shared interests or a clash of emotional needs. However, there is no doubt that it will enhance your chances of finding someone who may turn out to be a compatible partner.

The point about attractiveness is that, in itself, it has the power to draw people to you. After this, of course it's up to you, and this is where other kinds of 'attractiveness' may play a role. Moreover, although someone may lack conventional good looks, they may have other qualities or characteristics which prove to be attractive to others. A lively and original personality, for example, might operate as a magnetic force for potential partners. When we say that someone has personal magnetism or that they have charisma we are expressing the fact that others are drawn to them because of their special qualities or skills. On the one hand these qualities may simply be very compelling chat-up lines, or a smooth and charming way of dealing with situations where there is mutual sexual attraction. On the other hand, the possession of rarer charismatic qualities such as the subtle use of hypnotic suggestion, may also create the same effect. Of course such methods can also be used in the service of deception, manipulation and exploitation as well as for benign purposes. The murderer Charles Manson used the technique of hypnotic staring to mesmerize others and combined this with his bizarre (pseudo) philosophy-of-life, to bring them 'under his spell', so to speak, and motivate them to commit (multiple) murder on his behalf (Bugliosi and Gentry 1977).

More benign uses of these sorts of charismatic qualities and skills are reflected in the use of the term 'guru' when it refers to a someone with a particular expertise or specialist knowledge. Thus there are so-called economic, political and scientific gurus, who attract a group of loyal supporters around them. Philosophical, religious or spiritual 'gurus' also trade on their exclusive possession of 'arcane' or mystical knowledge. Such people benefit psychologically from their power to attract supporters. Approval, self-affirmation, a sense of achievement and significance, and so on, are the kinds of emotional and psychological pay-offs that flow from such 'attractors'. Quite clearly this gives such gurus a great deal of influence and control over their supporters or followers, and again this can be put to benign, or exploitative, or even evil purposes. Because natural leaders like this seem to possess something beyond the reach of the normal mind, people are willing to trust and put their implicit faith in them. This uncritical allegiance makes the power of the guru over her or his followers especially compelling, as well as being fraught with potential dangers associated with the abuse of such power.

But we are all gurus in our own small ways. We tend to lead with what we regard as our best personal qualities in order to impress those we wish to notice us. We all have little ploys – although we may not use them consciously or intentionally – to draw particular people to us. For example, you might have an endearing smile, or infectious laughter, know a lot about music or dancing, or maybe you're an excellent cook or good at telling stories. As ever, of course, there is no guarantee that we will be successful when we try to impress or influence someone.

Disappointment is a normal part of the game of life, and what we consider to be our own 'attractors' are no exception to this rule. Nevertheless, when we are successful (even if only partly) in bonding with someone who interests us, the emotional and psychological rewards follow close behind. As with the 'professional gurus', the experience of being able to draw people towards you by personal magnetism alone creates and reinforces positive feelings about yourself.

Seduction

I am using the word 'seduction' in a much wider sense than usual. It's normally associated with sexual activity and more often than not, with the idea of sexual predation, as in the description of someone as an 'expert seducer'. In this sense it is also connected with being led astray (as in the phrase 'being seduced into a life of crime'). However, seduction actually refers to anything that tempts, beguiles, entices or allures. So in fact, you could even be 'seduced' by the smell of coffee!

In relation to benign control, seduction is about satisfying your emotional needs by employing tactics that tempt, entice, or lure the other person into providing them. This is not necessarily something consciously (or cynically) planned as such. It might simply be a regular part of your usual way of living and coping. Also seduction can work in tandem with the use of attractors. For example, physical attractiveness or a charismatic personality may be involved as part of an overall strategy of seduction. But seduction is also a distinctive form of benign control in its own right.

Whereas attractors are qualities or attributes which, in themselves induce others into your orbit, seduction demands rather more deliberate effort to make it work effectively. It depends on the ability to carry through a plan of action designed to achieve a particular goal. The goal of course, being linked to some emotional or psychological need. Seduction may take many guises though they all rest on a foundation of 'soft' or gentle persuasion, allure or enticement.

Charm may be used as an instrument of seduction. Although charm can be associated with 'smarminess' which in turn can be linked with false flattery, deception and manipulation (as for example in women abuse), it also has a more innocent meaning. It is about the power to attract, fascinate or arouse admiration. Thus charm may be used to gain an agreement or to influence others into consenting to the charmer's wishes. Gentle powers of persuasion which require the skilled use of communication, conversation and behaviour may be brought to bear on the 'target' in a manner which is irresistible for them. The target is enticed by implied promises or sweeteners, such as 'I'll love you even more' or 'I'll love you forever if you do this for me'. Other things such as loyalty or trust may be pledged as part of the exchange. Typically the charmer will use appeals to the inner person by using intimate knowledge of them. For example, 'I know you don't like my mother, but it would make me very happy if you tried to get on with her'. A personal appeal like this gains its force through the implied suggestion that the charmer 'will be very favourably disposed towards you, if you make this effort to make him or her happy'.

Of course, such appeals could slide into a kind of emotional blackmail if used inappropriately, but nevertheless the exchange of emotional gifts lies at the heart of seduction. Thus, 'pressing the right emotional buttons' makes seductive appeals even more effective. Pressing emotional buttons entails targeting the 'right' emotional vulnerabilities or sensitivities (those that really open up the person's psychological defences). But also, *the way* you ask for something, or promise or demand something counts just as much as what you're asking for, in encouraging the response you want.

You may adopt a particular tone of voice (humourous, babyish, sexually seductive, parental, fake formal), in order to touch the other's feelings, or make them remember a special shared experience. You may simply inject humour into the situation as a way of creating a congenial or co-operative atmosphere. In your conversation you may include key phrases or invoke lover's talk or pet names to increase the intensity of your appeal. Referring to shared knowledge or experience strengthens bonding and commitment and makes persuasion easier.

Similarly the kind of facial expression you adopt, the amount and quality of eye contact you maintain with the person all influence the outcome. That is, it's not just what you say, but also what is communicated non-verbally that is essential to seduction. The overall effect is to project yourself as a certain kind of person, one who is to be trusted and is sincere and genuine. Apart from this aura of trustability, other attractive features may be part of your natural repertoire of behaviour. For example, the use of humour inserts an atmosphere of light-heartedness into proceedings.

In a similar vein, teasing, flattery and gentle sarcasm may also be appealing to others. It's important to use judiciously (what you know to be) your greatest powers of attraction. This is because seduction only really works when the other person feels as though they are on fairly equal terms and can effect the outcome. They don't want to feel pressurized, threatened or intimidated by someone who is all too willing to use their power against them. It must be remembered that in the right circumstances, revealing one's weaknesses or vulnerabilities may prove to be more appealing than overt power. Being vulnerable *may* (depending, of course on the personalities involved), bring out the protective and caring side of the other person and thus make them more willingly compliant.

Striking bargains

Although seduction often involves the mutual exchange of emotional gifts, such exchanges are usually unspoken and occur below the surface of the relationship. In striking bargains, mutual control is achieved more explicitly and openly. But because it is benign control, it's not about deceiving or manipulating the other person. Rather, it involves achieving a working relationship in which there is mutual satisfaction. However, unlike seduction, each person is more aware of exactly what they need to contribute to the relationship.

In this sense striking a bargain is clearly defined. For example, a husband and wife with a couple of young children may decide to take alternate days off from childminding in order to pursue their independent interests, such as going to the gym, going out for a drink with friends, or participating in a sport and so on. In this way the bargain is almost of a formal nature – 'we agree that you'll do this if I do that'. It's not that the arrangement is entirely without emotional content or psychological implications. Of course, if the bargain begins to break down because one or both parties flout the 'rules', then emotional conflict may well ensue.

It is different from seduction in that the bargain is clearly acknowledged and understood, rather like a pre-nuptial contract, although not necessarily written down. Of course, where a bargain is unwritten, people may have different recollections and opinions about what the bargain really meant or what the rules are. Seduction, on the other hand, is based almost wholly on an emotional understanding which, by nature and deliberate choice is rather fuzzy and ill-defined. Many bargains, by contrast, relate to fairly straightforward practical matters such as who does what, when it comes to housework, or turn taking at childminding.

However, some bargains have a further, more interesting complication. On occasion people agree to support each other emotionally to cover over flaws or weaknesses in themselves or the relationship. For example, where one of the partners in a marriage is uneasy talking about intimate emotional matters, their partner may tolerate this in exchange for equal tolerance with regard to their own anxieties about socializing or social situations in general.

It might be argued that this kind of relationship is basically unhealthy because it is based on the apparent weaknesses of the individuals involved. However, it could also be understood as mutually supportive. As long as both partners are aware of the real nature of the relationship and are getting what they want or need from it, it corresponds more to a benign arrangement than a stolen or exploitative one. Although the benefits obtained seem rather negative in that they prop up mutual weaknesses, it could be seen in an alternative light. Misguided though they may be, those involved are also motivated by care, support, empathy and co-operation. No one within, or outside the relationship is exploited.

This is very different from a relationship in which partners pledge loyalty to each other to hide criminal behaviour or to maintain economic advantages (such as a luxurious lifestyle). For example, a wife might tolerate her spouse's infidelities in return for her own 'independence' and access to his economic and other power resources. She might remain 'loyal' to her husband (in public terms at least), even when his exploits have been publicly disclosed. Both partners have guaranteed protection from outsiders who might threaten the advantages or benefits they gain by remaining loyal to each other. Especially in the case of public figures or political leaders, the deception of the wider public involved in such bargains makes it a threat to morality and democracy.

People skills

A great amount of genuinely benign control involves the use of people skills. That is, knowing and understanding human behaviour so that you are able to both give and receive something positive from relationships. This usually centres around the exchange of emotional support, sympathy, humour, companionship and so forth. People skills target the emotional essence of social bonds and so directly attend the core emotional needs I outlined in Chapter 2. The mutual use of people skills energizes the bonds that connect us with others.

Nevertheless, even if the arrangement is only one way, perhaps because one person doesn't have the skills, or is unwilling to employ them, it can be a force for good. This is frequently the case in social or probation work, or work with the mentally or physically disabled. Often clients resist the interference of the professional case-worker. Fear and lack of trust may prevent the client from responding positively to encouragement or support. Thus they resist doing what is best for them. However, despite this, the consistent and sensitive deployment of human relations skills by the professional may eventually establish trust and rapport with their client.

Having good people skills means that you are aware of the sensitivities and emotional needs of others and can manage them in a manner that allows both them and you to get something from the situation. For example, if you know that a person is angry, it's unwise simply to threaten them or say that they've got no reason to be angry as this will only make matters worse. If you have good people skills you will know that the best thing to do is to try to take the heat out of the situation, by acknowledging their anger and showing them that you understand why they are angry. In this sense you are taking their point of view and seeing the situation as they see it. This makes them feel supported and understood, rather than isolated and rejected.

People who work in service industries (such as flight attendants, nurses, teachers), must possess people management skills because they often have to deal with members of the public who are frustrated, fractious, complaining or aggressive (Hochschild 1983). It is important that troublesome clients or customers are dealt with sensitively so they can continue to do their jobs with a minimum of hold-up or fuss. But such skills are just as important for us all in our everyday lives and personal relationships, because they allow us to have our own needs met at the same time as we 'manage' other's emotional sensitivities.

Among the many different varieties of these skills, some are of crucial importance. Being able to listen to what others are saying seems deceptively easy, but good listening skills are much rarer than might be imagined. It's not just a matter of physically hearing what is being said, rather, it's about gaining a real appreciation of another's thoughts, feelings and intentions. Part of good listening is allowing space in conversations for others to express themselves, rather than using the conversation solely as a means of expressing your own thoughts and feelings. However, listening is not simply passive, it involves getting the other person to elaborate on what they say and to probe sensitively a bit more when they seem confused or reluctant to reveal their feelings. Good listening is also about responding to people by really taking into account what they are saying. Understanding what someone really means requires more than knowing what the words themselves mean. Empathy, or being able to put yourself in someone else's shoes and being sympathetic to their point of view, or situation is essential for properly understanding them. This is not only a sort of practical appreciation of their overall circumstances and emotional needs, but also involves a moral and ethical standpoint. Empathy, means being able to appreciate another's physical and emotional pain in a way that doesn't exploit, or deceive them. In essence the ability to empathize is what distinguishes the average, healthy citizen from those psychopaths and sociopaths who commit violent murder and/or mercilessly torture other humans.

True empathy, requires the ability to accurately 'read' other people's motives and emotions. The clues to these things are not always apparent in what people say. Their non-verbal behaviour is often more important and revealing. Whether people stare, or avert their eye's when talking with someone of higher status reveals something of how they think of themselves, whether they are socially anxious and so on. To a person skilled in reading another's non-verbal behaviour, such observations provide invaluable help in understanding and dealing with them. Apart from eye contact, things like facial expression, bodily posture, hand and arm gestures, are all clues as to a person's real feelings even if they verbally express something different.

Related to this issue is the importance of picking up the unstated messages or meta-messages (Tannen 1987, 1992) that other people are sending out. These are messages that comment on the nature or 'state of play' of particular relationships. This is particularly important in intimate relationships, where those involved have an interest in maintaining the closeness and trust invested in the relationship. For example, many couples or sexual partnerships founder on this issue. Comments like 'we always used to go out for walks together', may seem harmless enough at face value. But in the context of a relationship going through a 'bad patch' it may be that the one who is saying this is trying to convey the meta-message that she, or he, is concerned that they are drifting apart from each other.

Chapter Summary

- Self-identity and desire are expressed practically in terms of different styles, types and strategies of interpersonal control.
- 'Stolen' control (as in emotional blackmail) and 'exploitative' control (as in women abuse) are attempts to exert complete control over their 'targets' or victims. The perpetrator's self-interest is paramount.
- Benign control caters for the mutual interests, rights and needs of others. It is essentially co-operative, always partial and flexibly adapts to unfolding situations and relationships.
- Benign control is essential for the formation of intimate relationships like love, friendship, neigbourliness and dealing with and managing people at work or in service transactions.
- There are different styles and strategies of benign control: attractors, seduction, striking bargains and people skills.

5

Inner Power and the Higher Self

Chapter Preview

- The links between the self-help and personal development literature and notions of inner power and spiritual growth.
- The mistaken assumption that all control is negative, 'bad' or exploitative, countered by the view that benign control is a positive and ubiquitous force in social life.
- Social interaction facilitates ethical behaviour, but also provides opportunities for deception and manipulation.
- The close links between the 'higher' or spiritual self and the everyday self.

This chapter centres on the notion of the 'higher self' and I want to reinforce my claim that it is an important component of the self (although it may remain a latent and unused capacity). However, much of the literature on spiritual growth and personal transformation that explicitly supports it, has a simplistic and erroneous view of the overall nature of the self. In particular it has neglected and misunderstood the essential role of the social components of the self and how the higher self fits in with this more complex vision. Many of the writers of the literature have suggested that getting in touch with our higher selves and freeing our inner power is only possible if we stop trying to control others. As a result we are thereby able to live healthy, peaceful and fulfilling lives.

I shall look at some of the arguments for this view and then go on to suggest that in the light of the arguments already outlined in Chapters 1–4, this is a mistaken and partial viewpoint. It fails to grasp that power, mutual control and control over others are essential ingredients of social life and that without it we would be ineffective in our dealings with others and vulnerable to manipulation and exploitation. In particular, mutual, benign control is necessary for real spiritual growth and, in fact, healthy personal relationships can only be maintained by taking this into account. I conclude by offering some brief remarks on the relation between the higher self and the everyday self. Let me first outline the general arguments of those who believe that control over others is a bad thing and must be done away with in order to achieve spiritual growth and true inner power.

Personal transformation

Modern life is often a stressful experience in which people feel that things are beyond their control and they cannot affect the course of their lives or the events and circumstances which impinge upon them. Whatever the immediate cause of distress, much of it centres on feelings of personal powerlessness, low self-esteem, insecurity and anxiety. During the past twenty or so years an enormous amount of psychological, self-help and personal development literature has sprung up around these issues. It is designed to address such problems as how to regain control, or build self-confidence or develop the skills necessary for self-empowerment.

Many of these books are themed around the fundamental problems that people routinely face in life. For example, do you feel a nagging sense of dissatisfaction even if you are a successful individual and why? Why do we often feel that something is missing from our lives and that things don't make us happy for long? (Ashner and Meyerson 1997). Books on self-help and personal transformation offer hope to people who somehow feel downtrodden by the general trials and tribulations of life, or who are not maximizing or fulfilling their potential. In tackling such questions and providing useful tips for coming to terms with them, this literature promises to enhance the quality of people's lives by suggesting ways of boosting self-esteem, security and confidence.

Such books are fundamentally about how to achieve a level of personal effectiveness which will enable you exert some influence on a world that seems to be controlling you, or which you experience as threatening and oppressive. Thus the literature covers a fairly wide range of issues to do with psychology and interpersonal relations. For example, one author enjoins us to 'stop being a victim' and shows how to 'enjoy your life your own way, without being manipulated' (Dyer 1979). The same author also guides us towards 'the way to your personal transformation' (Dyer 1998). Rowe (1988) invites us to make the best of ourselves by becoming 'truly successful as a person' and 'developing the personal and social skills we lack' instead of continuing to live our lives feeling 'in some way trapped and oppressed, frustrated, irritable, haunted by worries and regrets'.

These books aim at a radical assessment of a person's inner core with a view to the gradual evolution, improvement and reshaping of self-identity in tune with the changing circumstances of our lives. In this sense the self is viewed as something which may change flexibly over time, rather than as fixed and trapped in an unchanging personality. However, to be able to change or evolve requires that we have some awareness of who we are and how we project ourselves. We need to be able to reflect upon who we are and to imagine what or who we might become if we chose to evolve. Additionally, of course, we need the skills to make the changes that we wish to make, and these are essentially what the self-help and self-improvement literature endeavours to provide.

Understanding the self as a project that can be worked on, improved and up-dated in this manner allows us the possibility of achieving a level of self-mastery. In turn, it is promised that this will allow us to make a more significant impact on the world around us. However, such techniques of self-improvement should not be thought of as egotistical or a narcissistic indulgence. Although these same techniques could potentially be misused or exploited, in this context they are linked to a 'moral' programme. In this respect self-improvement techniques are focused not only on the individual, but also aimed at the betterment of our relations and dealings with the social community as a whole. This is underlined by the fact that in many (though not all) of these books there is a high spiritual (as well as moral) content which underpins the advice that is offered. In this sense the existence of a spiritual dimension is consistent with doctrines aimed at restoring feelings of authenticity, peacefulness, clarity of mind and purpose, and acquiring or regaining the capacity to love yourself and others. In short, it is about gaining some control over your feelings and thoughts about reality.

Taking control of your life

A very influential book in this regard, and one that typifies the genre as a whole, is Susan Jeffers' *Feel the Fear and Do It Anyway* (1987). In it she argues that the main barrier preventing people from 'moving ahead with their lives' is the feeling of fear when we take a chance or do something new and challenging. Thus we become stuck in our 'comfort zones'. The way to become unstuck is to feel the fear but to push through it regardless, thereby taking more control of our lives. However, being able to take control is only possible when other things are involved. For example, letting go of negative thoughts, developing self-esteem and adopting a positive attitude to all life's problems. Also, taking control requires being more assertive and powerful within, being able to deal with resistance from others, having purpose and meaning, creating trust and love and experiencing more enjoyment.

The key to handling the fears that we have about the outside world – what happens at an interview, in your new career, what your partner, friends or children are doing – does not lie in controlling these external events. For Jeffers the way to diminish fear is 'to develop more trust in your ability to handle whatever comes your way' (Jeffers 1987, p. 16). This is linked to the notion that 'you are the cause of all your experiences *of* life, meaning that you are the cause of your reactions to everything that happens to you' (p. 51). In this respect people must take responsibility for their experience of life in order to be more powerful in themselves – to be in control. From this perspective it is no good complaining that you've got a lousy job, or that you are in a destructive relationship, or that your son or daughter is driving you crazy. In reality it is you who are *choosing* to be in that relationship or that job. It is you who is letting other people act in this way towards you. Until you acknowledge that you are responsible for the choices you make, then you will not realize that it is you who is causing your own unhappiness or lack of joy in life. Although it might not seem so at first sight, this in fact is a blessing because if you know that you can create your misery 'it stands to reason that you can create your own joy' (p. 51).

Being in control of your life means fully understanding that you create what goes on in your head. Taking responsibility in this regard involves not blaming others or yourself for what happens to you, or how you feel. It also requires silencing the voice of negativity that accompanies most of us most of the time. Further, taking responsibility means recognizing the psychological pay-offs that keep us stuck in situations that we would rather leave. Consider for example, the pay-off of not having to face the possibility of rejection by searching for a new job, or the pay-off of gaining attention by always being sick. Finally, being in control requires being aware of the many choices of action and feeling that you have in any situation and choosing the one that involves your growth and peace of mind.

Breaking the habit of negative thinking and replacing it with a more positive frame of mind is essential to these processes. So too, is breaking away from unhealthy ties with loved ones and encouraging healthier ways of relating. Relinquishing the need for approval from loved ones (say your parents) allows you to establish strength and independence and gives room for personal growth. Replacing childlike (approval seeking) relationships with more adult ones (where you take responsibility for your own actions) allows you to act more lovingly.

Pushing through fear

Crucial to dealing with the fears that prevent you from taking control of your life is the issue of decision-making. Being more in control of your life requires understanding that there are, in fact, no wrong decisions for you to make. Making a mistake is not really possible, since we can all learn from mistakes. Also, it is important to be aware that every decision you make provides an opportunity to learn, grow and find out who you are, no matter what the outcome.

This links with the idea of getting rid of negativity in the sense that the more you say 'yes' to what the world has to offer, you will be able to explore new opportunities. Instead of resisting change you will tend to focus on the new pathways that are opening up. Although you cannot control the world, you can control your reactions to it. This requires that you always act positively no matter what the situation. By so doing, you will hold back feelings of helplessness and hopelessness and instead, believe that you can create meaning and purpose 'in whatever life hands you' (Jeffers 1987, p. 61).

A theme in Jeffers' book, but which also appears in many others is the importance of giving, trusting and loving in order to eradicate fear and live a life of joy and satisfaction. Being able to give your love, time, thanks, information, praise and so on, to others in a genuinely altruistic manner allows you to feel better. There is a distinctively spiritual aspect to this since the message is about becoming less selfish and more concerned with the well-being of others. The point is to give without any expectation of receiving anything back, instead of operating on the basis of a 'hidden barter system' (p. 170). There is nothing wrong with receiving back as long as there is no prior expectation about getting something in return, which gets in the way of giving in the first place. Of course, at the same time we actually do get something back; we get a sense of satisfaction, an absence of fear, an ability to reach out to others rather than remain huddled-up, nursing our own insecurities and selfishness. The wider point is that we get back what we send out. If you give out love, you will receive it back.

The more you worry about what you will receive in return, the more fearful and manipulative you will become. This creates a need to control others so that you will not feel short-changed. Of course this merely breeds resentment and anger. The only way forward is to be prepared to give unconditionally because this endows you with loving power. Fear and indecision are transformed into confidence and positive action. Thus, the sequence is, inner power is created (control over your reactions and acceptance of your responsibilities) which in turn, destroys your fear and the need for external control and manipulation of other people.

Inner power

Clearly, the authors I have referred to are all agreed that a true experience of your own self involves being in touch with your spirit. Making such a connection means that you are not unduly influenced and swayed by external things such as situations, circumstances, events and people. You are not constantly seeking approval from others or anticipating failure or rejection. You are not coming from a position of fear based on the need for approval and the need to control external things. Instead of this false, ego-based external power, you will possess true inner power which fears no challenge, has respect for others and feels beneath no one. Importantly, self-power 'magnetizes people, situations and circumstances to support your desires' (Chopra 1996, p. 13).

Inner or 'true' power thus imbues you with qualities that will increase your satisfaction and fulfillment in life. By giving unconditionally – that is without expectation of receiving something in return – peace of mind and contentment will follow. Unconditional love, in particular, is a key component of the inner power which encourages bonding with others and derives from true knowledge of the self. Conversely, always expecting something in return for what you give is operating from a basis of fear and is ego-based.

According to the authors mentioned here, the trouble with the ego-based self is that it is preoccupied with self-interest, need and allaying fear. As a result it is negative and manipulative and is solely concerned with the question 'what's in it for me?'. The ego-based self is never fulfilled, and often feels empty, bored and dissatisfied with life. By contrast, the notion of a higher or true self is concerned with universal energy flows and is the source of positive thoughts and actions. The higher self is loving caring and joyful. It reaches out to others and acts in the service of humanity as a whole. Everyone possesses a higher self but is not always in touch with it. It takes a degree of attunement and sensitivity to be able to connect with it on a regular basis.

However, once in touch with your higher self you have access to a universal energy that flows from within you and renders negative energy harmless. You act from wisdom and feel good inside (Roman 1986, p. 149). Accessing the higher self is a way of tapping into a source of power which will lift you out of a negative, complaining, mind-set which languishes in a victim mentality. The higher self will propel you into a world of abundance and light. You still may feel that you cannot control many of the things that happen to you, but being in touch with your higher self gives you power to control your experience of the world.

In short, you are able to control your responses to the things that happen to you. Thus you may transform your world by choosing to see joy and peace where formerly you may have felt only misery and discord. Clearly, the notion of a higher self fits very comfortably with the other elements of the self-help and personal development psychology, particularly inner power and the idea that we can choose our personal reality. This whole philosophy of being speaks to a vast number of people who believe themselves to be spiritually under-nourished and lacking the basic resources to make life satisfying or fulfilling.

That is, this literature is about providing the tools with which a person may exert some control over their lives in a world which constantly threatens to get out of control, to obliterate or overtake them. In a sense it addresses the fact that the normal circumstances of everyday life create a pressure to be in control of yourself and your reactions to others. Being able to create a personal reality which is inherently satisfying staves off feelings of alienation, boredom and emptiness which are often a feature of modern life.

Benign control as an essential and positive force

In the context of the arguments already set forward in this book a great deal of what has been said above flatly denies the importance of control and the role it plays in social life. The self-help and spiritual growth literature assumes that control is unnecessary, inherently bad and should be eliminated for the sake of a more peaceful and loving world. Such a view fails to take account of the distinction between benign, stolen and exploitative control. Benign control enables you to be effective in relation to yourself as well your dealings with others. It is an important tool used for establishing bonds with other people and of creating co-operation, love and support.

In this sense benign control is essential to social interaction and is very different from manipulation or exploitation. Every time we interact with another we naturally and automatically use benign control. It is a basic part of our effectiveness in dealing with other people. We try to influence others in order to get them to do what we wish, but at the same time we satisfy them by recognizing their needs and caring about their well-being. If we were unable to influence people and events in this way we would not be human beings but unthinking, unfeeling automata.

The self is complex

In view of my outline of the constituent elements of the self in Chapters 1–4, the view of the person based on the distinction between the ego and the higher self is far too simple. It suggests that before we connect with our higher selves we are all ego and little else. The idea that we are only concerned with manipulating others to serve our needs, is both pessimistic and unfounded. The fact is, we do not live alone in the world, as if we were separate egos isolated from each other. We live in a social world and we are connected with each other through our relationships and the need for co-operation. We have to take others into account whether we like it or not. This role is fulfilled by parts of the self concerned with engaging with social life and interpersonal relationships.

The fact that we have to live with others and co-operate with them to some extent ensures that our behaviour cannot be entirely selfish (egotistical), with a complete disregard for other's feelings and interests. Of course, some individuals are more self-centred than others. However, we often support and 'care' about each other in everyday situations because we trust and feel positive towards our fellow human beings. Much of our behaviour is altruistic and ethically underpinned. But this is not necessarily because of religious or spiritual motives and thus cannot be said to be entirely the work of the 'higher self' (although, of course, the higher self may feed into it).

The rules of interaction

There are more down-to-earth reasons for our ethical behaviour. Importantly, there is a set of moral rules about how we should treat others in our everyday enounters with them. These are not written down, but everyone knows what they are, and generally complies with them. For example, there are 'rules' about being polite in company, or about when to make a contribution to a conversation, or how to make small talk or chit chat. There are unwritten rules about how close we should stand next to people, about how much eye contact we should make with others in different situations and so on. Very often these rules, for example, about appropriate amounts of eye contact, or for interrupting someone, are not known by any specific name or label. However, without ever explicitly talking about the rules themselves, everyone seems to know what is 'right' or 'appropriate' behaviour for the situation at hand. As a result we tend to conform to the rules without really thinking about them.

Mutual trust and respect

When people come together face-to-face they tend to treat each other with mutual respect. It is only in special circumstances – such as when a row develops or deception has occurred, or when there is chaos and conflict in society – that this mutual trust and respect breaks down. In normal circumstances we tend to believe in the sacredness of the individual, that each of us has the right to be treated respectfully and with due care and civility (Goffman 1967). In routine daily life we generally take people at face value and don't go out of our way to embarrass them, or make personal criticisms. It is only when someone breaks these rules and expectations themselves, that we feel at liberty to do the same. This highlights the fact that although these obligations towards others are generally altruistic, they are not entirely unconditional. The respect, care and regard for others that features in our daily lives is a product of our social nature. It is a kind of unspoken collective understanding that we will treat others with respect and civility in the hope and expectation that we ourselves will be treated similarly. So it's not for entirely selfless reasons that we behave 'ethically' in this manner. It has more than a little to do with our own concern to be treated fairly and with due attention to our own 'sacredness' as individuals.

Self-care and protection

It is clear that we do not always behave like selfish egotists manipulating others for our own purposes. We do many things unselfishly with a true regard and concern for others. In part this is because we depend on others for providing our self-esteem by treating us with due regard for who we are as individuals. But self-esteem, self-confidence and so on are also created by our own self-attitudes and the way we treat ourselves. We have to be protective and self-affirming in order to maintain a basic level of self-confidence and psychological security.

We cannot afford to be overwhelmed or fatally wounded by a thoughtless stray comment, criticism or gesture. To be over-sensitive in this respect would make us too vulnerable to the routine buffeting of social encounters. Clearly then, we have an important responsibility for maintaining our own self-esteem. So we have to distinguish between self-regarding or self-affirming behaviour which reinforces our confidence and security, from truly egotistical behaviour which aims primarily at dominating or manipulating others.

I'll give to you if you give to me

The idea that inner power and the higher self are based on pure unconditional love seems to be more of an ideal than a realistic or attainable goal. In this sense, the notion of giving love without expectation of receiving anything in return seems rather naive. If we only helped somebody because we anticipated payment, or some kind of gift or an equivalent favour in return, then that would certainly be conditional, manipulative and self-serving. However, although we might not expect anything from the other person in return for caring or neighbourly behaviour, it is not really true to say that we receive nothing in return. Unselfish behaviour like this always carries with it some intangible psychological reward such as inner satisfaction, fulfilment, peace of mind and so on. This does not make the behaviour any less well-meaning or unselfish, but it does undermine the myth that we expect absolutely nothing in return. OK so the reward is awarded to, and by ourselves, so to speak, and not necessarily by another (although a simple 'thank you' may reinforce a feeling of doing a good turn). OK so we don't receive money or ego-enhancement as a result of our behaviour, but we do receive spiritual nourishment and the opportunity for inner growth.

That these are subjective and intangible feelings should not blind us to the fact that they are priceless in comparison to any material or ego rewards. Nor should it obscure the fact that spiritual rewards are *rewards* that we anticipate even if we don't expect them. This, surely, is the whole point of such behaviour in the first place. That this kind of behaviour makes us feel good about ourselves and our relations with others is a compelling reason to repeat it in future. After all, if we felt nothing, or worse as a result of our selfless behaviour (being kind and thinking of others before ourselves), there would be little or no incentive to do it again. In this sense a particular style or pattern of behaviour needs to be rewarding *in some sense* before a person will adopt it as a regular part of their behaviour.

Inner power and benign control

Much of the personal/spiritual growth literature is rightly geared towards the empowerment of individuals. This inner power is created when a person has built up their self-confidence and self-esteem. As a result inner power banishes fear and insecurity and in turn, rids you of the need to control and manipulate others. Now there is certainly room for a view of power that stresses its softer, beneficent other side. This indeed, is what my notion of benign control is designed to address – where control is understood as the active side of power, or 'power in action'. However, I think it is a mistake to view power as something which only has an 'inner' existence, as if it was solely about 'private' individuals cut off from the rest of the world.

As I have stressed we are *social* beings and, as such we are always involved in relationships and can never be free of their influence. Thus part of our sense of inner power has to be about being sure of our ability to deal with others. Therefore, inner power always has an unbroken connection with the outer social world. This world of social interaction is concerned with influencing and controlling other people's responses to us, while they attempt do the same. To be able to participate in this mutual dynamic depends on our effectiveness and skillfulness at dealing with and managing other people. At heart this is how you make someone respect you, love you, or even just notice that you exist! But it is not just one way.

You can only influence or control other's responses or behaviour by taking into account their needs, personality, moods and situation. Similarly, it is the way in which people respond to you, with love, suspicion, anger and so on, that helps to build up and reinforce your subjective power (your confidence, security and so forth) in the first place. In this sense there is no such thing as inner power independent of the way you actually use it in your daily encounters. Inner power is always tied to your experiences with other people – in the outer social world!

The social nature of the self

The self-transformation literature with its emphasis on a spiritual or higher self as against the ego, and the notion of 'inner power' as opposed to control over others misses out some fundamental social aspects of the self and its link with everyday life. Compared to the model of the self outlined in Chapters 1–4 this is too simple a view. It needs to be amended to take account of the role of these social aspects. We require some idea of the effects of our daily interactions in order to understand properly how the different aspects of the self relate to each other.

Instead of simply thinking about the ego versus the higher self we have to add in the idea of the social and existential dimensions of the self. The social aspects of the self are concerned with you and your interactions with family, friends, partners, officials and so on. Thus the general focus is not simply about you as a unique individual (ego) or about your relationship to a universal spiritual energy (the higher self). In this sense the social dimensions are excluded in the writing on self-transformation.

There will always be tension between egoistic desire and social responsibility. Whether you choose to behave badly towards others, attempt to deceive, manipulate or control them for your own ends will depend on what kind of person you are. If you are interested in the 'rewards' that bad or criminal behaviour may provide, your egoistic (selfish) behaviour will be projected onto your encounters with others.

However, as social beings we are dependent on others for a host of things and so there is always some pressure towards co-operating with others. After all, at times even criminals need friends, lovers, mothers, fathers – as well as victims! Obviously, if you are generally well-intentioned in the first place you will see things less selfishly and view people from a more trusting and caring perspective. The point is that social interaction encourages ethical (morally correct) behaviour as well as providing an opportunity for deception, exploitation and manipulation. In this sense ethical behaviour does not only stem from the higher self.

Ethical behaviour and control

This is important because the self-help and spiritual transformation literature does not seem to recognize the social–ethical parts of the self. Instead, it gives the impression that the worldly self is entirely contained in the ego. Furthermore it insists that the ego is inherently manipulative and controlling and only the higher self is concerned with the well-being of others. But social interaction requires some level of mutual respect and trust between people. Ethical behaviour is reflected in the tendency for people to help each other out and give moral support. Examples of this are, refraining from unnecessarily embarrassing others, encouraging them to get through difficult situations, or repairing damage done by a thought-less comment. Such behaviour has the effect of making encounters go smoothly without undue or pointless conflict. At the same time this ethical behaviour is also a product of our willingness to take our social obligations and responsibilities seriously.

Social obligations and constraints push us in the direction of ethical behaviour – irrespective of whether we actually behave in this manner. There is a whole range of social behaviour which tends to be altruistic and benign but which is not simply the product of some spiritual dimension. (Although of course a spiritual influence may make this tendency even stronger.) This is where control, particularly the benign type, fits in. To some degree, depending on the individuals and the situation involved, all social relationships involve mutual (benign) control.

A competitive struggle for power and energy?

The short answer to the question 'Is life a competitive struggle for power and energy?' is sometimes it is, and a lot of the time it isn't. When it's not, it's more like a mutual exchange of energy and a ritual celebration of our bondedness with others. It is a mistake to view power (and hence control) in blanket terms, as if *all* control was competitive, manipulative and unethical. A good illustration of such dangers can be found in *The Celestine Prophecy: An Experiential Guide* (Redfield and Adrienne 1995).

This very popular book outlines nine key (and hitherto allegedly 'secret') 'insights' into life and also provides a guide to your own personal adventure. Indeed, by using it as a guidebook and grasping these insights sequentially, we are meant to move towards the establishment of 'a completely spiritual culture on earth', and to 'explore a deeper connection with your own personal energy and divine source'. Let me say at the outset that although what I have to say is critical in nature, I also think that the book has many good and important things to say about human existence and potential. My criticisms focus in particular on the 'fourth insight' which is concerned with 'the struggle for power'.

The authors state that the 'fourth insight tells us that humans compete for energy with each other' and that 'we do this unconsciously in every encounter' (1995, p. 83). By struggling for control we ward off feelings of fear abandonment, pain and so on, that were originally developed in childhood. We win energy by using 'control dramas' through which we make up for an accumulated deficit of attention, self-esteem and self-worth. Power struggles and conflict occur when we realize that we are losing energy because someone is manipulating us.

Our habitual way of gaining attention and stealing energy is by enacting control dramas. These are fixed ego positions that we have developed over time because they have proved their worth in getting what we want. The authors identify four main ego positions that we use to manipulate others and steal energy in a control drama. Intimidators rely on aggressiveness, loudness, and appearing to be dangerously out of control in order to get their way, whereas interrogators use hostile criticism and finding fault with everything others do and say. Less aggressive is the aloof strategy which depends on being distant from others, not asking for help and avoiding commitments. The most passive strategy is the poor me or victim who pulls attention to him or her self by making others feel guilty, say by crying or viewing everything negatively. They exude vulnerability but are not interested in solutions.

We need to release the need for control dramas in order to feel a psychological lift. By seeking to manipulate or dominate the other's attention we become weak and insecure and cut ourselves off from an 'inner connection' with 'mystical energy' (Redfield and Adrienne 1995, p. 94). If we engage in struggles and conflict over control, our minds and thoughts tend to dwell on these things and this creates anxiety about the need to be in control. Furthermore, a preoccupation with controlling others cuts us off from our intuition, creativity and spirituality. Surrendering control is the key to becoming aligned with universal energy (p. 109). Once we understand that we are depending on control as our 'only way to make things happen our lives miraculously open up' (p. 93).

Is this a realistic picture of human behaviour?

Emphatically no, this is not a realistic picture because social life is not always like this. Of course, it is true that some control is like this, and that control dramas do exist. However, it is misleading to imply that this is what social life in general is like. This is far too pessimistic a view of human nature and also fails to take account of the crucial role of benign control in our everyday relationships. The kind of control dramas that Redfield and Adrienne identify only account for a small proportion of social life.

It's not that these control dramas are unimportant. However, these are instances of control going bad, they are unhealthy forms of control. In order to understand how control goes wrong in this manner we must view it as a deformed or perverted version of benign control. Thus when we consider the underlying roots of social behaviour and how it is formed, we can place the significance of control dramas and the competitive struggle for energy in a wider perspective. In this sense they are exploitative forms of control which are a part, but by no means the whole of social life.

Given the importance and pervasiveness of benign control in social life it is crucial to avoid understanding human behaviour and social encounters as primarily concerned with stealing or competing for energy. A more accurate picture of benign control is produced if we understand it as a mutual exchange of energy. Sometimes this exchange is unequal, sometimes not, but it is the to-and-fro, give-and-take nature that underlies the process. Instead of struggle, conflict and competition, we should think of it as a process of bonding and the establishment of the kind of rapport that enables each person to get something out of the encounter. Yes, the jostling and jockeying for turn-taking or talk space that arises in conversations and encounters may, at times, take on a competitive edge. But this is always in the context of a mutually agreed convention of give and take, and the exchange of responses (gifts) between all those present. It cannot be construed simply as theft, or a struggle for dominance.

In addition, control must not be contrasted with creativity as if the two were incompatible. All social behaviour is creative to some degree since it involves mutual adjustments in relation to circumstances which are constantly changing. In encounters people are continually coming up with improvised responses that suit the unfolding situations in which they find themselves. Since control is an example of social behaviour it too involves varying levels of creativity.

Rather than cutting us off from our intuition, creativity and spirituality as Redfield and Adrienne claim, benign control *actually requires* creative and intuitive solutions to the problems that arise in dealing with, and managing people in everyday life. This issue is connected with an even more basic one about the way we make things happen in our lives. The authors say that we depend on control as if it were the 'only way to make things happen' (p. 93) and that we need to surrender the need for control in order to become aligned with, and tap into, universal energy.

However, as we have seen, they make no distinction between types of control and hence they don't understand the absolutely crucial role of benign control. 'Inner' or subjective power is reflected by, and in, your ability to make things happen. Your power is your ability to engage in the ebb and flow of encounters so as to give and get what you and others desire. In short, self-efficacy and effectiveness in dealing with others in this way is essential for making relationships work in the interests of all concerned. The idea of surrendering your control in this manner does not make sense. How could it when it means surrendering your effectiveness (and a significant chunk of your inner power) as a skilled, competent social actor?

Self and social life: for a more sophisticated view

The basic problem with Redfield and Adrienne's ideas is that they are based on the unquestioned assumption that all control is negative and has negative consequences. Such a view simply does not do justice to the intricacies of social life in which people control in subtle, complex and benign ways. Nor does the negative view appreciate that the psychological and social processes involved have the effect of cementing human relationships. By understanding the role of benign control and influence we come up with a much more inspiring vision of the mundane world, or at least, its potential.

An unfortunate fact of life in the modern world is that exploitation, domination and manipulation do play a significant role in many areas. Naturally, it would be naive to think that they did not affect our lives in many ways, even if only indirectly. Also, although many of us have no direct involvement in this kind of crude and negative behaviour, we can never claim to be entirely free from the influence of less serious forms of selfishness or manipulation. In this respect our social lives are played out against the backdrop of a mixture of positive and negative motives, emotions and intentions. Even though you may be a genuinely caring person concerned about the well-being of others, most likely you will occasionally fall prey to selfish, ego-responses, or at least, to some kind of self-protective behaviour.

Nevertheless, more often than not, human social behaviour is influenced by moral and ethical strands which underpin the vast amount of civil, co-operative behaviour that characterizes everyday life. How then, does this relate to the higher self, inner power and spiritual growth? My intention has not been to deny the existence of a spiritual dimension, rather, I have been concerned to highlight the importance of the social dimension (self and social interaction) as a *complementary* source of ethical standards in human behaviour. That is, this social source of inner power and personal growth reinforces many of the benefits that derive from connecting with the spiritual energy of the higher self.

This is partly because the rules and guidelines that govern the internal world of social interaction have the effect of tempering the selfishness and manipulative drives of the ego. At the same time these same rules tend to push us towards a concern with ourselves in relation to others and the obligations that go along with them. As I've pointed out, these 'involvement obligations' (Goffman 1967) centre on the care and maintenance of the self – whether it's you or someone else. However, mutual trust and respect, the sacred character of the individual, the use of tact and so on, are also important.

So, although they stem from different sources, the concerns of the social and higher dimensions of the self converge over many issues of interpersonal ethics. This does not, by any means, undercut the importance or necessity of the higher self and spiritual growth in general. However, it does indicate that these areas are not the only source of ethical standards that underpin people's behaviour. What is missing from the self-help and spiritual growth literature is a recognition of the importance of the mundane world as complementary source of 'spirituality' and interpersonal ethics. There is room here surely for the influence of a secular as well as a metaphysical spirituality.

In the light of these concerns more generally, the issue cannot be about getting rid of all control as Chopra (1996) and many others argue. Benign control is a natural and essential part of social life. Without it we would be unable to attract and keep our relationships since it is a central means for satisfying our need for bondedness with others. Lacking this ability there is every chance that we would become isolated, alienated and potentially dangerous outsiders.

The higher self and the everyday self

In the light of these considerations what then can we say about the higher self and its relation to the everyday self? Although the rules of everyday social interaction are a potential source of ethical behaviour that may underpin the higher self, this is not inevitable. For each individual, contact with their higher self is a potentiality which may or may not be realized. Actual engagement with the higher self depends more or less on deliberate effort and conscious choice. Why some individuals rather than others choose this path is a complex question which I cannot pursue here in any great detail. However, I would suggest that the core of the issue is linked to the question of personal meaning.

Thus the higher or spiritual self is not a manifestation of spiritual need as such. That is, at least in the first instance, it is not the result of innate and specifically spiritual needs pushing towards expression. Rather, it is about the quest for personal meaning and how this may be satisfied. As language-using, cultural beings the need to make sense of the world and our place in it is a particularly strong impulse in us. But the question of personal meaning can be resolved in a number of different ways including, but not limited to, the adoption of an interpersonal morality associated with the higher self. This is why the realization of the higher self is best understood as a human 'potential' which may remain latent unless deliberately cultivated and embraced. To see this in perspective consider the alternatives to the higher self as the basis of personal meaning. If the higher self is not actualized or engaged then the question of personal meaning must be resolved in an exclusively pragmatic, secular manner. That is, it will remain unattached to a moral framework with an overriding emphasis on care for fellow human beings. There are two broad possibilities associated with behaviour flowing from personal meaning detached from such a moral framework.

First, an amoral or agnostic attitude towards others (and oneself) may lead to a kind of moral 'neutrality' in a person's behaviour. While this may not necessarily entail destructive and anti-social consequences, the moral vacuum is always in danger of tipping behaviour in this direction. Thus behaviour will sometimes err on the side of care and compassion while at other times, on the side of manipulation and tyranny, in a quite arbitrary manner. Second, an amoral position can lead directly to behaviour which is consistently anti-social or criminal. This in itself represents a large swathe of possible activity ranging from relatively minor forms of manipulation such as emotional blackmail and psychological pressure, through to varying degrees of domination and coercion.

By contrast, engagement with the higher self serves the need for personal meaning by tying it to an ethical–moral framework. As a result behaviour and attitudes towards others are underpinned by the values of care, compassion, empathy, understanding, trust, love and so on. Importantly, as I've stressed through this chapter, such values may be fostered through a secular morality engendered by social interaction (or the 'interaction order' as Goffman describes it), as well as through an explicit commitment to otherworldly, purely spiritual ethics. Thus engagement with the higher self is not necessarily limited to those who are dedicated to the pursuit of explicitly spiritual practices, it is a possibility open to those whose behaviour is socially benign in intention as well as in consequence.

Chapter Summary

- The self-help and personal transformation literature stresses the link between the eradication of egotistic desire and the development of inner power and spiritual growth.
- By branding all control as 'bad' or 'negative' this same literature overlooks the positive and ubiquitous role of benign control in social life. Similarly, the view that the self is purely egotistical in nature is naive and underestimates the complexity of the social aspects of self-identity, some of which are altruistic in nature. There is a need to distinguish self-care and self-protection from egotism.
- It is inaccurate to characterize social interaction solely as a competitive struggle for power and energy. Not all control is manipulative and unethical. Ethical behaviour is intimately related to social life and the social aspects of the self as well as explicitly higher or spiritual concerns.
- Benign control is a mutual exchange of energy which has the effect of affirming human bonding and the establishment of rapport. It requires creative and intuitive ways of dealing with people in everyday life. Although exploitation, domination and manipulation exist in the modern world, moral and ethical strands underpin a vast amount of the civil and co-operative behaviour of everyday life.
- The higher self is born out of the need for personal meaning rather than spiritual need. Thus it is a potential in us all, but may remain latent in those who find personal meaning in a pragmatic amorality. The higher self may manifest itself in mundane social interaction. It is not exclusively informed by otherwordly or spiritual concerns.

6

Relationships
and Their Dilemmas

Chapter Preview

- Self-identity resides in the intersection between psychological (subjective) reality and social reality.
- Self-identity emerges and unfolds as it confronts and lives through dilemmas of behaviour and problems of life. The core dilemma of separateness versus relatedness.
- The undisclosed, private self and the normal asocial and anti-social sides of the self.
- Communication, intimacy and self-identity.
- Desire and relationships.

Personal identity is forged at the intersection between two distinct but overlapping universes or realities, that of individuals (psychological reality) and that of society, or social reality. These realities are interdependent – one couldn't exist without the other – but at the same time they have their own distinct characteristics. That the self is created in the subtle, combined effects of these different but connected realities has, more often than not, been overlooked.

On the one hand, psychologists and philosophers have tended to emphasize the self as emerging exclusively from individual or subjective factors (attitudes, cognitive and mental constructs, instincts, innate motives, personality traits). On the other hand, sociologists and cultural commentators have tended to see the self as a creation of purely social forces (such as norms, values, discourses, class, gender). Both views overlook the complexity and subtlety of the relationship between individual and social realities, as well as how their distinctive characteristics (or properties) differently influence the creation (and renewal) of the self in everyday life.

In this chapter I argue that as individuals, we experience tensions and strains on our identities and social relationships which are a result of having a stake, and being in both worlds (universes or realities), at the same time. The two realities exert pulls and pushes on us from opposing directions while we (try to) make decisions about which direction we want to go in. This tension and opposition between the two universes impacts on both our personal relationships and self-identities by constantly confronting us with behavioural dilemmas.

Further on I suggest that there are a number of dilemmas to be considered, but it is perhaps useful to see them initially as offshoots of one basic dilemma – that between 'separateness and relatedness'. The core relevance of this dilemma is that it directly reflects and represents the two realities of the individual and social universes. The 'relatedness' side of the dilemma represents social reality in so far as social relationships are the stuff of society and social reality. Conversely the 'separateness' side reflects the unique subjectivity of the individual.

It can be readily appreciated that this dilemma plays a central role in all our lives. Sometimes we wish to be more apart from others, to have our space, to collect our thoughts, to feel free. At other times, we want to join in with the crowd. If we feel rejected by a group or an individual we usually yearn to feel more included and not so separate. In other situations we might feel that other people expect too much of us, always wanting us to do what the group does, or what they want us to do and we secretly wish that we could have more independence. Thus the idea of being separate from others as against being closely entwined in relationships (relatedness) represent the opposing pulls of individual (psychological) and social reality.

Such dilemmas are relevant to questions of personal identity and behaviour in general. They prompt us to ask questions and make choices about how we *should* behave, who we are, and what we want to make of ourselves. Thus such dilemmas make us think about questions such as 'Who am I?' or 'What kind of person do I wish to become?' Or we consider issues such as How closely do I want to become involved with particular people (friends or romantic partners)? Do I want to cool down my relationship with my parents and spend more time on my own? Do certain of my relationships seem oppressive and stiffling? Do I feel trapped in an unhappy relationship? Does my most intimate relationship make me feel alive?

The dilemmas are usefully described as existential in that they concern problems in living and the nature of everyday existence. The dilemmas are existential in that they are about the immediate practical problems that we face in our daily lives – how to behave, what to say or do in particular relationships and situations. (In the next chapter I deal with what might be described as deeper existential questions about what life means and how we feel about the world in general.) If we accept that the dilemma of separateness and relatedness is the primordial or core dilemma in this regard, there are several others that are linked to it, but which emphasize rather different aspects of life and behaviour. The ones I focus on in this chapter are:

personal *v* social
private *v* public
separateness *v* relatedness
independence *v* involvement
aloneness *v* togetherness
personal space *v* intimacy

If we take the viewpoint of the individual who must deal with any of these dilemmas in their personal life, the problem is of balancing a particular choice (I want to be alone) against social demands (there's a lot of pressure on me to do what they want). But this not so simple because in the balancing act, the individual acts as an agent of control. The person asks themselves questions such as: To what extent am I able to make a free choice? How much control do I have in this situation? Can I obtain what I want or need, but also satisfy my partner?

The extent to which the person is able to get away from a destructive relationship, or transform a situation in which they are uncomfortable, is crucial and depends on the amount of power they have. Whether a powerful individual allows someone else to have their own way depends on the extent to which they are prepared to relinquish some of their own control and influence. Clearly control is also wrapped up in emotional issues. Having the power or leverage to break free from an oppressive relationship obviously has implications for a person's quality of life and emotional satisfaction. A relationship in which both partners are satisfying each other's emotional needs is one in which there is a relative balance of power and a mutuality of interests (mutual benign control).

Relationship dilemmas and the emergent self

The existential dilemmas are basically about what we make of ourselves in the world. They are about who we are, and who we are in the process of becoming, as well as how we live our lives and the quality of our relationships. In this process the self is both the medium and the *outcome* of engaging with the existential dilemmas. Thus feelings about ourselves (our own sense of who we are), and our behaviour towards others helps to shape the way we respond to, and deal with particular dilemmas. For example, at the begining of a close, loving relationship you may have a need for more personal space than your partner. Your preference will affect the way you behave towards and negotiate with your partner about this issue. You may want to have your needs accommodated while also respecting your partner's needs. This will guide your (mutual) efforts to achieve the right kind of balance in your relationship between personal space and intimacy. But the very achievement of this balance may prompt you to be more understanding of your partner's greater need for intimacy. As a result of dealing with this dilemma you may develop into more tolerant or understanding person.

The self is in a constant process of becoming as it successively confronts and emerges from the problems of life. This emergent self continually feeds back into our feelings about life, and so on, and helps to shape the manner in which we deal with the next set of existential problems and dilemmas that we encounter. Emotional struggles of more or less intensity may accompany the sometimes painful evolutionary stresses that the self undergoes. In this sense, a person may experience much uncertainty and confusion about personal identity.

Egoism and altruism

We have all come across people who could be described as insufferable egoists or selfless martyrs. But on the whole, the average person would fit somewhere between the two extremes, at times expressing their caring, altruistic side, while at other times, veering towards an unrealistic assertion their own self-importance. However, the choices involved are never that simple. The fact that the choices preclude and contradict each other is a problem in itself. Because of it, most of our encounters with others require that we must weigh up the likely consequences of pursuing either the path of self-orientation or that of altruism.

Leaving aside those who have extreme personalities (rampant egotists or obsessive altruists), in practice we usually resolve this dilemma by responding on a decision-to-decision, moment-to-moment, or encounter-to-encounter basis. That is to say, the path we 'favour', and so the way we respond, will be decided *in situ*. In turn, this will be formatively influenced by our previous experience of similar situations, our judgements about the likely consequences of the possible actions we might take, as well as how we interpret and evaluate the situation.

In actual instances of decision-making – particularly on-the-spur of the moment during encounters – the self carries a double burden. We need simultaneously to have and to deploy elements of both egoistic self-interest and sociality (or other-directedness – a need to submit to the reality, rules and norms of the social order). So even though there is a tendency for us to be shunted either towards orientation to self or community (Parsons 1951), as individual selves it is necessary that we deploy some element of each in all our behaviour.

There are two aspects of this that are important here. First, as a unifying centre of awareness (Branden 1985) the self is neither inherently selfish nor altruistic, since we know that humans are capable of both kinds of behaviour. Until early developmental processes have got underway in the child, this centre of awareness is quite neutral. Before this space becomes occupied by a definite individual personality with a behavioural repertoire, it is simply an empty awareness-monitoring mechanism which has yet to be channelled in particular directions by social and psychological influences. Second, as I argued in the previous chapter, the egocentric aspects of the self are not only about selfishness but also about protective self-interest. In the absence of a protective armour of self-interest the self will rapidly lose its robustness and durability. A person whose psychic armour is weak is in danger of losing their sense of security, efficacy and competence. They may experience great difficulty and confusion around self-identity. In the worst scenario this might end in a nervous breakdown or mental illness.

It is important, therefore, that there is a membrane of self-care, and self-interest cocooning the self if it is to remain pyschologically healthy and socially effective. However, social interaction and personal relationships, equally demand some awareness of appropriate social rules and requirements, as well as some real, practical engagement with them. Thus there is a necessary duality within the self that has the effect of balancing-up a person's more general leanings to either side of the selfish–altruistic divide.

The undisclosed self: the private interior

Much of what we take to be our personal identities are on public display in some sense, more or less all the time. Whenever we appear before others we have to present them with some face or self-image. After all, they need to know what kind of 'beast' they are dealing with, whether they can trust us and what we are up to. Some such elements of identity are easy to spot: most egotists, for example, tend to make an overt display of their arrogance, superiority and assumed self-importance since their main aim is to make a visible point of putting others down, or at least, letting them know their place. Those who are naturally caring and compassionate are often less concerned with ensuring good public exposure of their character. Nonetheless, because they wish to make themselves available to those who need their ministrations, their caring and compassionate side is usually not difficult to observe. However, there are many aspects of self-identity which are not at all overt and observable. In fact many of them are the subject of deliberate and elaborate efforts at concealment, even absolute non-disclosure.

These undisclosed or private aspects of self-identity have often gone unnoticed, perhaps because of their invisibility and underground nature. (In this sense they are akin to the study of emotional phenomena.) Interestingly, even Erving Goffman, the sociologist who did most to champion the importance of the study of everyday behaviour (including self-identity), by-passed this topic and focused far more on public displays of social behaviour. Goffman was quite explicit about this omission, 'I assume that the proper study of interaction is not the individual and his psychology, but rather the syntactical relations among the acts of different persons mutually present to one another' (1967, p. 2).

Goffman is quite right to insist that a proper account of interaction cannot be wholly reduced to individual psychology and that the social dynamics of interaction have an emergent influence that derives from properties of social reality. However, it is a great error to then focus exclusively on a 'minimal model of the actor' as 'an individual *qua* interactant' in order to 'suit ... sociological study' (Goffman 1967, p. 3). This has the effect of squeezing the inner life out of real individuals and offering a very one-dimensional view of them in return for a supposedly 'proper' sociological account.

But this account cannot be properly sociological because it is a distortion and simplification of individual psychology and this error is then simply imported, like a virus, into the sociological account. Individuals are never simply interactants because they are always real, complete and unique in their own right. We miss out the subtle mutual influences between subjective reality and the social reality of interpersonal dynamics if we employ an impoverished, 'minimal model of the actor'. Goffman's position is typical of most sociological accounts. The importance of the inner reality of the person, their private enclaves, separate interiors, their asocial, anti-social tendencies are thus swept out of the account and rendered mute by their absorption into a social constructionism.

This is exemplified by the fact that Goffman insightfully distinguishes between front (public) regions of behaviour and back regions out of public purview (such as kitchens in restaurants). But significantly, he makes no equivalent distinction when it comes to the self. Thus for Goffman and many other social commentators there are no back (undisclosed or private) regions of the self that lurk behind their public presentation, at least not any that are important to a full and correct analysis and explanation.

The problem is that such a vision of human beings is artifical, not to say superficial. It almost wilfully neglects key aspects of the self which have an important impact on interpersonal behaviour. The following discussion then, is designed merely to indicate a range of behaviour that is germane to the private or undisclosed self. But it is also crucial to view it in the context of the dilemmas and tensions this private self sets up with its more public presentations. In this sense the importance of insisting on a full psychology of the individual is so that we don't lose an appreciation of the opposing tensions and forces of subjective and social realities to the black hole of social constructionism.

Private rules, preferences and lifestyle habits

It is almost commonplace to think of rules of behaviour as entirely social in origin and purpose. It is assumed that such rules exist for social and regulatory reasons because they actually function as guidelines for socially appropriate behaviour. But this overlooks the myriad of private, personal rules that we as individuals invent for ourselves which also impact on how we behave and our relations with others. Private rules in this sense tend to be personalized versions of more general social rules, practices and moral attitudes. So although in some part drawn from society, they are private in nature because of their individual customization. Also their privacy derives from the fact that more often than not they remain unspoken and undeclared as a person's subjective preferences, attitudes and practices.

Such personalized guidelines are relevant to the vast array of personal attitudes and behaviours. For example, they might cover conduct in sexual relations (including preferred sexual practices), the treatment of colleagues and friends, lifestyle preferences (fashion, eating, habits such as, drinking, smoking and drug-taking), personal pursuits, hobbies and leisure-time activities, personal finance, attitudes and rules about spending and consumption and so on. Almost every conceivable activity could be the subject of such personalized and uniquely tailored rules. In this sense each individual may be defined and identified by her or his distinct repertoire of behavioural rules, preferences, lifestyle habits and so on, which constitute a unique personal identity profile. These rules, preferences and lifestyle habits allow the person to avoid meeting situations cold. By being personally prescriptive in nature they ready the individual for upcoming behavioural decisions that may be required. They provide a bank of accumulated problem-solutions which allow a person to say 'no I don't do that in this kind of situation', or 'yes, I will do it, as long as the following conditions obtain'. In short they enable us to come up with pragmatic solutions to the moral and behavioural problems or dilemmas that we encounter in social life. Consider, for example, the following:

Sexual and partnership rules:
- I don't have sex with anybody on the first date.
- Whether I have sex depends on the situation and/or the person.
- I prefer sex partners who are very fastidious.
- Someone who is excessively fastidious is a turn-off.
- My partner must be happy with oral sex.
- I won't consider being in a relationship with anyone who can't talk about their feelings.

Money/finance rules:
- I always buy my own drink and avoid buying rounds.
- I always buy friends a drink.
- I don't lend money.
- I lend money to anyone who needs it.
- I only lend money to family.

Leisure time pursuits:
- Eating out is fun and I do as often as I can.
- Eating out is expensive and indulgent.
- A holiday means going to the beach every day and getting a suntan.
- A holiday is doing something challenging.

Emotional/feeling rules:
- I keep myself to myself. My emotional life is private.
- Conversations about personal feelings are dangerous and confusing.
- I like to be straightforward and say what I feel. It's best not to 'beat about the bush'.
- I'm not important enough to express my feelings.

Although such rules are uniquely customized they clearly serve the social function of allowing the individual to navigate through the frequent confusion of social life and personal encounters. The rules express the resultants of experience – the person is able to say 'This is what experience tells me is the case' or 'This is what works for me because certain things have happened in the past, that I don't like and I don' t want to repeat'. But the rule is about a projected future, of what might happen and it is an attempt to control the outcome. Sometimes such customized guidelines are closely related to a person's favoured lifestyle. In this sense they are simply expressive of style, or group allegiance and what is considered cool or tasteful. Unlike sexual and partnership rules they are less about providing moral solutions to behavioural dilemmas. For example, fashion preferences ('I wouldn't be seen dead in that!', 'I always wear high collars', 'Bermuda shorts are very uncool') express an individual's tastes and in so doing prescribe certain 'acceptable' habits while proscribing others. The decision to smoke or continue smoking is similar in that it is an expression of personal control over lifestyle decisions and preferences (Denscombe 2001). It announces 'I do this' or, 'I have this habit' and that's my decision, no one else's.

Thus there is a broad mix of different rules, preferences, lifestyle indicators and so on which perform different social functions but which all mark out the individual as as distinct personality in a social context which threatens to obliterate or at least obscure such individuality. They express the need for the separateness and distinctiveness of the individual so that he or she declares their significance and retains some distance from others while at the same time being a part of the crowd.

Generally speaking, these rules are not tightly specified in a formal sense. They are more like rules-of-thumb, broad guidelines. Some may be more strictly adhered to than others, especially if they are backed up by, or personal interpretations of, socially sanctioned rules, as for example, in sexual habits informed by religious rules about what is appropriate for an adherent or believer. More frequently, private rules are personal inventions or interpretations of more general behavioural rules. Thus the rules may have some flexibility built into them so that *ad hoc* modifications may be made. For instance, it may be a personal rule never to have sex on the first date, or with a stranger. But, if the 'right person' comes along, or if it genuinely, or intuitively feels right, then an exception may be made, or at least contemplated.

It is the fact, however, that these rules, lifestyle preferences and habits typically remain undisclosed that most clearly expresses the tension between the opposing pushes and pulls of the social (public) and subjective (private) orders. Its not that they have the status of 'dark' secrets which *cannot be* made public, but rather, that they represent the personal, private, interior life of the individual, which is not normally publicly announced or voluntarily shared.

When pressed, people may admit to this private order (particularly to intimates). There is usually nothing shameful, and often nothing embarrassing about the beliefs they represent. However such sensitive information has to be communicated with care, especially when it concerns feelings or information that may prove potentially explosive if emotional insecurities and vulnerabilities are involved.

What must be kept to yourself

Apart from rule guidelines, there is a whole class of private thoughts (information, attitudes, opinions, prejudices, emotional reactions and so on), that are most definitely not for public consumption. These things must remain unspoken, because they are socially unacceptable or inappropriate. The fact that these are disparaged socially and perhaps even subject to public condemnation if they inadvertently come to light, does not stop us from holding them. Some such thoughts, of necessity, are destined to remain forever a personal secret – such as the fact that you are regularly gripped by murderous thoughts and have killed several people already, or that you want to be unfaithful to your partner as soon as you get the chance. Others thoughts may be shared by a very restricted group of asssociates who can be relied upon not to betray the secret. Consider the following for example:

Prejudices (against types of people based on physical characteristics):
White males, blacks, females, long-haired types, males with facial hair, excessively thin or fat people, foreigners, old people, particular regional or national accents, loud and brash people, timid or shy types.

Sexual thoughts (what may be thought, but cannot be said on meeting, being introduced, or observing someone):
'I really fancy you'.
'You (male or female) have a sexy bottom (hair, eyes)'.
I really fancy your mother' (father, daughter, son).

On situations:
This is a really lousy party.
God I feel very uncomfortable having to make small talk, especially with someone I despise like you.
Haven't you got anything smarter to wear than that.

Feelings:
I hate you. But I'll never tell you to your face.
I'm going to get my own back as soon as I can.
I have loved you since the moment I first saw you (directed to your boss' wife/husband).

Many of these are negative and/or judgemental in character and that is one reason why they must be kept private or secret in the first place. But this kind of negativity is very much a part of everyday life even though ideally, the world would be a much better place without it. And it is surely true that those of us who are not spiritually perfect, or strictly politically correct (and who is?) entertain many such thoughts during a typical day, even if we censure ourselves for having done so.

It is also certainly the case that couples, close friends or relatives often 'enjoy' sharing prejudices (for example, collusive mockery of deformed or disabled people, of men with huge beer bellies, women with big breasts). There is also collusion of this kind regarding shared but 'private' preoc-cupations or traits for example, humour around toilet habits, belching, farting, swearing, unusual sexual practices and so on. Such topics of dis-cussion or humour are largely prohibited 'in public' but lead a comfort-able existence as part of the flourishing underlife of the self.

In the category of thoughts restricted largely to the self are those that cannot be disclosed even to your nearest and dearest. This reverses the idea that intensely private thoughts can only be shared, if at all, with those with whom you are most intimate or close. This category refers to things which you don't tell your partner, and things they don't tell you. For example, it is commonplace for one person to say to another (a friend perhaps, sometimes even a stranger) 'I do think my spouse, part-ner, lover, is wrong to take such a such a job', or that 'He/she reacts too strongly to adversity', or that 'She/he is obsessed with being success-ful'. These are usually accompanied by a rider such as 'But I could never tell them that'. The implication is that such an admission might cause serious emotional damage to their partner and possibly to the relation-ship itself.

Finally, there is personal knowledge that cannot be revealed without it undermining yourself to some extent. For example, even though you might be ruthlessly honest in you dealings with others it would be a weirdly self-defeating strategy to begin every encounter with someone new by declaring all your weaknesses and failings. Not only would this be for you a bad negotiating stance in general terms, but it would be an unnerving experience for the other person – inviting them as it does, to treat you as an inferior. In this sense we mainly keep discrediting personal information from others in order to sustain a particular image ourselves (usually the most favourable).

The asocial and anti-social self

That the phenomena discussed above refer to the notion of a private or undisclosed self and to its corresponding underlife, speaks to a broader area of experience in which the social and public sides of the self are, to varying extents, supressed. But to underplay the assertive elements of the self here would be an oversight. The self sometimes struggles and strains against the social order, the wider social consensus or social regulations, constraints, obligations and expectations that pressure us towards conformity. Part of the self's sense of its own power, efficacy and competency is lodged and manifest in just this kind of oppositional energy.

Self-identity, in this sense, is forged in the person's attempts to stave-off, or keep at bay the insistent demands of social forces and to preserve some enclave of privacy in spite of the enveloping influence of social organization (Crespi 1992, Layder 1997). It is not simply, as Wrong (1967) once argued, that sociologists tend to operate with an over-socialized concept of the person and neglect self-interest, sexual motives and so on, although they clearly still do this. It is also to do with imagining that pressure to submit to social processess remains unopposed by the individual's need to generate distance from them and thus to support a distinct personal identity. In this respect and in a decidedly minor key, we are necessarily unsocial, anti-social and deviant as an intrinsic part of our need to create and sustain a self-identity. A self-identity which endows each of us with a significance which depends upon, but at the same time actively counters, the absorbent, containing power of relationships and social organization. The tensions and oppositions between the private and public aspects of the self reflect this wider interdependence between subjective and social reality.

Craving intimacy and wanting space

Although all the dilemmas of behaviour considered here are in a strict sense never properly resolvable, in practice we try hard to do just this. However, in the end our efforts are futile because they are impossible to resolve for anything more than brief periods of time. This is mainly because a balanced response can never be finally secured or fixed – it is always a moving target. Behaviour in accord with one side or the other of the dilemma, automatically neutralizes any associated with the other side. This is exactly the case with separateness versus relatedness and involvement versus independence. For example, if you say to your partner 'I'm going out for a walk, I'll be back in about half an hour', quite reasonably, your partner might interpret this as a statement that you wish to go out alone and that they aren't invited. If your relationship was supposedly still based on intimacy and your partner is at all sensitive, he or she may be very hurt emotionally by this rejection.

In effect, your assertion of independence (or your right to be separate) sends out the message that intimacy, relatedness, involvement or inclusion are not on the agenda. Your partner may take this to mean that you no longer think that intimacy and involvement are important in the relationship. He or she may even conclude that this signifies a fundamental sea change in the emotional quality of the relationship – in short, that it is under threat or in trouble. In fact, you might not have meant to convey this meta-message of rejection. It might simply have been the result of your habitual mode of speaking in which you stress your self-reliance and your lack of dependence or anxiety about being alone. If your partner objects and explains that she feels rejected and hurt by what you said, you might respond by saying 'No I didn't mean that. I just assumed that if you wanted to come out for a walk you would say so'. This might not be enough to avoid damaging implications. Your partner may still think that you do not care enough to make the deliberate effort of inviting her. Furthermore, it may be very important emotionally for her or him to feel cared for and included through explicit verbal messages. She may still feel that the meta-message (not caring enough) that has been conveyed, does not bode well for the future of the relationship.

Conversely, if you always feel compelled to invite your partner even when you need or wish to have time and space to yourself, you may begin to feel that you actually have no independence, or separate existence from your partner. You may begin to feel stifled and resent being so closely involved with (or entrapped by), the relationship and this, in itself, may lead to a great urge to break free. The more that involvement and relatedness take precedence in a relationship the less will those involved have a real sense of their own independence and individuality.

If a person asserts their need for independence and autonomy, the more they will endanger bonds of connectedness, intimacy and togetherness. A move towards one side of the dilemma, creates an imbalance in your relationships. Thus characteristically, relationships are constantly on the move in and out of balance in relation to these dilemmas. This, of course, is part of the ongoing dynamic of relationships. They are constantly readjusting and accommodating to the changing needs and intentions of the individuals involved, as well as to the evolving, unfolding nature of situations and circumstances.

Self-identity and style of communication

Part of the behavioural dilemma here concerns how much a particular person identifies with, and adopts a particular style of communication.

That is, to what extent is an individual's self-identity bound up with a typical way of relating to the world, and using conversation, language and talk in a manner that reinforces this. Take the previous example about saying 'I'm going out for a walk'. Is the person who says this, doing so because he or she automatically thinks of themselves as fiercely independent. Do they typically prefer to hold themselves at a distance from others? Do they not get involved with people generally? Or was their remark simply a one-off mistake, a slip of the tongue?

Of course, this could occur by chance. But the point has been made (see Tannen 1987) that the use of conversational gambits are part of a particular style of communicating which reflects gender differences. Tannen argues that men and women typically adopt different styles of communication with men stressing the more independent style and women expressing the more involved one. This is because women on the whole value close social bonds and connectedness and therefore often engage in talk-for-the-sake-of-it (often without significant informational content) in order to send out the meta-message that the bond or relationship is valued in and for its own sake.

Men, according to Tannen, value their independence rather more than social bonds and relationships which seem to involve giving away some of their self-reliance and independence. They tend to think of relationships as vehicles through which 'information' is passed or exchanged rather than as valuable bonds or social ties in their own right. In a strictly general sense there may be something in the argument about gender differences in conversational style.

Certainly it may account for some of the problems, conflicts and arguments typically experienced by men and women – particularly in long-term relationships. One of these, for example, is expressed in the woman's complaint that 'he never listens to me' and the man's complaint that 'she always expects me to know what she's thinking without telling me'. However, I'm not convinced that gender difference is the most important point about communication style, nor indeed that we can say anything of great value about differences in personal identity between individual men and women in such broad and generalized terms.

It is quite wrong to view individuals as simple reflections of the wider social groupings to which they belong (in this case the gender groupings of men and women). To do so, is to make the drastic mistake of regarding individuals as the simple playthings and mouthpieces of collective social forces such as norms, values, discourses and so on. Although the social groups to which people belong strongly influence their behaviour (even if only by actively rejecting such group identifications), they can only provide a background of cultural resources which *may* be drawn on by individuals. (And this applies to class and ethnic groups as much as to gender differences.)

Individuals are intelligent and knowledgeable enough to make their own decisions about which features of culture they will adopt, or be influenced by. Surely the most important point about styles of communication is that it is possible for *anyone* to use any style of communication and that this expresses something about their unique self-identities as individuals. Thus individuals (men or women), who consistently use particular styles of communication are expressing an identification with particular modes of being-in-the-world – what I've characterized as independence or separateness as against involvement and relatedness.

Individuals who see themselves primarily as independent and who keep their distance from others, certainly gain the advantages that flow from 'defending' their own space. Among other things these include; freedom to choose what you say and do, as well as to decide about factors affecting your material and psychological well-being, and to give absolute priority to you own needs, irrespective of other's. On the other hand, excessive self-reliance and independence is achieved only by relinquishing the rewards of social involvement such as a sense of belonging, inclusion, being cared for, and supported by others emotionally and materially.

Those who place more value on connectedness and bondedness with others have the benefit of a social network of support and care. As such they have at their disposal a communal safety-net which will be put into operation whenever their own sense of security, self-esteem, confidence and general spirits are at a low ebb. Without such communal support and insulation the individual is very vulnerable to emotional lows and depressive responses, even to the smallest upsets and crises in their lives. This is the case with people who are excessively self-reliant, or too proud to accept help, or don't want to 'bother' others with their 'trivial' concerns. Typically, these people already possess low self-esteem and feel unimportant and insignificant in comparison with others. Their situation is simply exacerbated by a privatized, independent stance which impedes any potential flow of help or support that may actually be on offer by the community. By avoiding social interaction the individual reduces even further the communication of information that may otherwise alert others to their plight. By remaining isolated and unnoticed such individuals often escape the safety-net provided by natural communal support mechanisms.

In relation to this problem of isolation it would seem psychologically healthier to err on the side of relatedness and involvement than rugged independence and stubborn individualism. This is especially the case in so far as the emotional and spiritual aspects of the self are more regularly monitored and more easily maintained within the context of close social bonds. However, it is also true to say (and this further highlights the insolubility of the dilemmas) that excessive enmeshment in close-knit networks and social bonds has its own problems. Notable among these are a relative lack of individual freedom, or at least a strong pressure to comply with the standards and values of the group. As long as a person naturally feels very insecure and uneasy without a close partner or friend or without a strong, supportive network then this is fine. It is probably more important to remain sane and secure than to complain that you don't have enough personal or private space. Nevertheless, as I've pointed out, such constrictions of personal space can be experienced as over-whelmingly suffocating. And if there are only very limited opportunities to express your individuality or to claim 'time-out' and personal space, then this may result in an emotionally explosive response.

Communication, intimacy and the self

As the foregoing illustrates our general style of communication is closely linked to feelings and emotional needs. It is important for the individual to be minimally tied into social relationships as a source of self-esteem and basic security. However, the connections between emotion and style of communication run even deeper. Not only is the social relateness (and involvement) side of the dilemma of crucial importance in shoring up basic security and self-esteem, it also feeds into general emotional skills and emotional intelligence.

Together, emotional skills and intelligence are themselves pre-conditions for establishing emotional attunement or intimacy with others. Emotional attunement refers to the way in which we are able to understand each other at the level of feeling. The extent to which we are attuned to each other depends on our ability to correctly identify and understand another person's moods, feelings and emotions as they unfold during our time spent with them. This may be a limited period as in a single encounter, or it may cover the whole span of an relationship.

Those whose style of communication emphasizes the skills of social relatedness and communal solidarity are already better equipped to achieve emotional attunement on a regular basis. Of course, it takes more than one person to create shared attunement, so the fact that just one person is skilled in this manner doesn't guarantee that attunement and genuine intimacy will occur. In fact in many personal relationships there is an imbalance of attunement skills (such as empathy, sensitivity, intuition, correct emotional recognition and so on), and this is often the cause of conflict, tension and failure to achieve intimacy. These interpersonal problems usually occur because the partners concerned are using different styles of communicating and this leads to misunderstandings. Because they fail to understand what the other is really saying they begin to devalue each other's thoughts and feelings. They may end up not even bothering to listen and just assuming that they will automatically disagree. For example, if one partner is communicating in a style which assumes that involvement, togetherness and closeness are the most important things, then it could be misinterpreted as a threat by the other partner whose style of communication stresses the value of independence and their right to have their own space. So if people use different starting points and assumptions for communication they are likely to misunderstand each other. And this is not a superficial problem that can be resolved simply by talking through issues at greater length. Unless there is some recognition of the different styles, and the assumptions they are based on, further talk aimed at clarification will fail and may even lead to more serious misunderstanding. Only by understanding your partner's style of communication, and taking acount of it, are you likely to avoid such routine communication problems. Unfortunately, this is all too rarely the case, and inadvertantly, much emotional damage may be done as a result.

The main point about this kind of misunderstanding is that it is never simply about not being understood in the literal sense of knowing or grasping what is meant, or even agreeing about a certain issue. Every social interaction is, to some degree or other, about emotional understanding and rapport (what is felt rather than said) and it may often be more important than cognitive understanding. If an encounter touches directly on an emotional or intimacy issue such as whether, or how much, you care for someone (or they care for you), then obviously the emotional component will loom large.

Non-verbal signals, meta-messages and intimacy

Even when the topic of conversation only seems to concern factual information, emotional messages are simultaneously being transmitted which comment on the state of your relationship (or how you are getting on with your partner). The *way* you speak to your partner (roughly, tenderly, patronizingly, respectfully), the sort of non-verbal signals you make (amount of eye contact or avoidance of gaze, your facial expression, whether and how you touch each other), all convey an enormous amount of information about the way you feel about each other.

The non-verbal signals, the meta-messages they convey and the way each person responds to them, are very important in shaping the fortunes of an intimate relationship. Emotional attunement and rapport – the feeling that you are in tune with each other's moods and emotions – is highly dependent on each person's ability to recognize and correctly assess the meaning of such non-verbal signals and messages. Good rapport and attunement, in this sense, is confirmed by your ability to accurately know, or intuit what your partner (or another person) is actually saying (or meaning), when conveying these things to you.

In the final analysis this means that to achieve attunement and rapport you must be sensitive enough to recognize the 'hidden' messages of rapport talk, and how to respond appropriately. You must know what these extra verbal messages mean or say about your relationship and how you're getting on with your partner. For this you have to decipher what is really *meant* by your partner, rather than simply hearing and registering the words that they utter. What is said and what is meant may be very different, and that is why the accompanying non-verbal signs (facial expression, and so on), must also be taken into account.

In short, it is only if someone is fairly skilled in handling social relationships that they will be able to really create and properly engage in emotional attunement. This means that only those who are able to deal generally with the relatedness and involvement (closeness and togetherness), side of the action dilemma will be able to achieve true emotional attunement since this requires the ability to deal with meta-messages. An important implication is that if someone overvalues their independence, self-reliance and separateness from others, or has never learned the skills involved in achieving real bondedness and rapport, then they may find themselves more or less trapped in one side of the dilemma. Being limited this manner they will be barred from achieving true emotional attunement and intimacy because they can cannot experience it themselves or recognize it in other people. It follows that such people may be permanently unable to achieve a normal or healthy degree of emotional intimacy. A person who is able to achieve real intimacy must have a firm grasp of the skills associated with social relatedness and involvement.

Of course, the average person will have at least some relationship skills but at the same time be able to operate separately and independently without any difficulty. They will be able to move relatively easily and appropriately between the different modes of being and different events and situations. By operating flexibly in this manner neither their independence as unique individuals nor their involvement in social life will be permanently compromised. Nevertheless, a person's basic rootedness in, and engagement with, the full potentialities of life (as indicated by the depth to which they are able to achieve emotional attunement and rapport), remain dependent on the skills and capacities of social relatedness and involvement. A person who is obsessed with themselves or self-absorbed will remain largely disengaged and detached from social life and interaction.

On this account genuine emotional life is only realizable through skilled and sensitive social involvements which permit the creation of a sharedness of feeling and empathic understanding. And of course this kind of attunement will be impeded by excessive attachment to egotistic/narcissistic concerns. However, independence and egotistic selfishness are not necessarily the same thing and the two should not be confused with each other.

A person may decide on living fairly 'independently' for a number of very different reasons. Some of these may well be to do with a sense of superiority or grandeur while at the other extreme other indivduals may opt for this as a means of defence or survival. Of course, an incurable egotist who is arrogant, pompous and self-important will have little room, if any, for generosity of spirit, care and compassion for others, and so on. In fact, all those qualities necessary for the achievement of emotional attunement will be in very short supply.

On the other hand a person who lacks confidence, has low self-esteem, or a social phobia may be 'forced' to be self-reliant and distant from others. Their apparent independence may be their way of avoiding stressful social situations and coping with the phobia. However, the longer such a state of affairs exists, the more embedded will the avoidant behaviour become. He or she will then have even less chance of acquiring the necessary social skills and confidence to enter fully into social relationships.

Aloneness and togetherness

The opposition and natural tension between aloneness and togetherness is a 'normal' routine feature of social life. Sometimes we wish to be alone (have our own space), while at other times we may have an overwhelming urge to join with others in some shared pursuit. In normal circumstances there is no problem in switching between the being alone mode, and being together mode.

However, sometimes aloneness may be transformed into its pathological form of loneliness. In this case the normal positive value placed on having some time or space to yourself, becomes displaced by the negative experience of enforced or involuntary aloneness. Frequently a person becomes lonely because they are unable to create or maintain social bonds or attachments to others. Such loneliness can be the end result of a process of exclusion by others. This may take several forms and may be caused by either defensive or offensive behaviour on behalf of the victim or sufferer of loneliness.

First, take the example of someone who is lacking in confidence in social situations and who would prefer to avoid them, if at all possible. Unless this person voluntarily takes measures (such as therapy), or is forcibly encouraged to do so by a friend, partner or family, then their preferred tendency to avoid problematic situations rather than confront them may well become completely entrenched. In so doing, of course, they simply exacerbate current feelings of aloneness (being cut-off from others) and convert them into to more definite anxiety and loneliness, perhaps ultimately, to a pathological state of isolation. Another possibility concerns a person who is, for whatever reason, overly aggressive, argumentative or irritable towards others. Instead of withdrawing or avoiding social contact themselves, as with the underconfident or shy, in such cases it is *other people* who initiate avoidance and withdrawal from social contact with the offending person. So much so that they may eventually be the deliberate target of exclusion, as sometimes happens in cases of paranoia. The individual becomes cut-off from communication and feedback from others and as a result cannot rectify his or her behaviour accordingly. A vicious spiral of exclusion followed by further paranoid aggressiveness may occur from which the individual is unable to escape. The final possiblity concerns the overly egotistical and arrogant individual whose splendid isolation results from their lack of generosity towards others. Their inability to recognize and (emotionally) reward other people's contributions and efforts has the eventual effect of driving people away and withdrawing their support. The rampant egotist, in this sense, allows little or no room for the care and cultivation of other people's emotional lives because his own occupies all the available space.

Clearly, to this extent egocentrism and the need to appear superior hinders the development of healthy adjustment in so far as it puts a break on real emotional attunement and rapport (based on equality of give and take). Thus, some kind of dampening down of self-interest, and self-absorption must occur before attunement can emerge. Ironically it is often the very people who are caught in the trap of excessive self-regard and self-importance who lack the attributes that might help drag them out of the mire. In this sense emotional attunement requires critical self-reflection, insight and sensitivity, a desire and willingness to connect with others, as well as those diffuse skills associated with empathic understanding itself.

The question of self-identity and its robustness is of great importance with regard to the dilemmas of aloneness and togetherness and of personal space and intimacy. I've already pointed out that these dilemmas represent, as it were, the normal or healthy alternatives that are current in everyday life. However there are two other possibilities which represent what we might call 'pathological' alternatives. These are the problem of 'isolation' on the one hand (and which we have touched on briefly under the guise of loneliness), and 'merging' on the other.

Isolation and merging indicate two equally deadly problems for a person who experiences levels of uncertainty, insecurity and confusion around self-identity. Although Laing (1969) suggested that this is a problem that schizophrenics in particular suffer from, most of us have, or will experience similar, but less acute problems from time to time. This is chiefly because they refer to generic experiences resulting from the double-faced nature of everyday social life. In this respect isolation is the end-product of a process of increasing aloneness that has eventually become out of control. This will have typically started as a means of avoiding difficult social situations caused by insecurity lack of confidence, low self-esteem, or social phobias such as shyness. For someone who is chronically fearful, anxious, inept or underskilled in a social sense, isolation may be tolerated or even preferred for varying periods of time. However, in the long-run the strategy is self-defeating because we are dependent on other people to sustain our sense of self-identity.

Social confirmation of identity helps stabilize our own sense of who we are. But social responses also influence the evolution and development of self-identities as our experience widens and deepens. Even though a person may prefer to remain in his or her own space for lengthy periods, too much isolation will have the effect of destabilizing self-identity, rather than preserving it. In this respect social contact is necessary to generate a sense of membership, belonging and inclusion. Other people provide us with a confirmatory sense of identity that we may not be able to provide for ourselves.

However, problems associated with merging, express the 'unhealthy' flipside of togetherness and intimacy. In this sense a person's uniqueness and individuality is threatened by the feeling that their identity is being dissolved by, and absorbed into, other people's. The separateness, individuality and autonomy of the self becomes blurred (and hence undermined) by a process of merging with others that is seemingly beyond the individual's control. We may experience this in a mild sense when we feel that the sheer weight, 'importance' and presence of other people is almost overwhelming. We may feel lightweight and of little consequence as compared with the seemingly large-scale and substantial character of other people or the social event of which we are a part. Normally, such feelings stem from momentary lapses of confidence or self-esteem and are quickly restored. However, the more insecure a person already is, the more likely are they to experience direct social contact as a real threat to their autonomy and self-identity. In this light merging with others is dangerously close to the annihilation of the self altogether.

Desire, relationships and the emergent self

We are never 'given' or finally 'completed' as individuals. Our personal identities are ever in the process of becoming, emerging and evolving. This is the main thrust behind this discussion of the behavioural dilemmas. Over time as our lives and personal relationships unfold we encounter problems connected with the need for intimacy versus the need for space, our preferred style of communication, selfishness versus altruism, self-protection versus vulnerability, emotional disclosure, attunement and intimacy, the ability to deal with other's emotions, and so on. It is important for each of us to strike the right kind of balance in our personal relationships with respect to these dilemmas. If we fail to do so then it will be harder for us to function healthily. In order to achieve this we have to continually adjust and realign ourselves with respect to these dilemmas and the existential problems which give rise to them. As particular problems, crises or life-events arise we have to juggle with the balances between various dilemmas. For example, you may decide to make more effort with regard to intimacy with your partner, or create more personal space for yourself as a solution to a particular relationship difficulty. However, care must be taken that any re-adjustment creates just the right new balance of mutual feeling. Unless it is done with due regard to emotional tone and attunement between the partners, it may simply store-up additional problems further down the line. Continual re-adjustment, re-attunement and renewal of rapport must occur in relation to life problems as they arise and as they impact on relationships.

In the absence of such emotion and identity work there is a great likelihood that the relationships themselves will become unhealthy, strained and soured. Those involved may also be affected psychologically, particularly if they are emotionally vulnerable in the first place. Unfortunately the self or personal identity will bear the brunt of this pressure and the person may become disturbed, or emotionally wounded as a result. In this sense, the ordinary circumstances of everyday life typically require successfully negotiating the thin line between healthy mental functioning and mental disturbance or illness.

Chapter Summary

- The tensions between the subjective interior of the self and the social exterior are reflected in real life action dilemmas.
- The basic dilemma is between separateness and relatedness but there are a number of others that are intimately connected to it, such as private versus public, independence and involvement and personal space versus intimacy.
- Self-identity is in a constant process of becoming as it engages with, and emerges from, life problems and existential dilemmas such as that between egotism and altruism.
- It is crucial not to dismiss individual psychology as important to understanding the self in social interaction. This is a mistake common to most sociologists. But this loses sight of the pivotal struggle between the opposing forces of subjective and social realities. The problem is 'lost' by being sucked into the black hole of social constructionism.
- Also lost is any reference to the private undisclosed side of the self as expressed in private rules, habits and lifestyle preferences.
- There are close links between style of communication, the self, and the opposing needs for intimacy and personal space. This underlines the important role of meta-messages in emotional communication and the need to achieve a balance in personal relationships with respect to behavioural dilemmas and life problems.

7

Personal Worlds and Private Feelings

Chapter Preview

- Self-identity and the engagement with deeper existential questions such as the search for authenticity.
- Feelings of 'aliveness' or 'death in life' and the problem of the dislocated self.
- The problems of meaning and existential aloneness. Confronting 'nothingness'.

This chapter focuses on perceptions and feelings about the nature of life and the world in which we live. Of course, these issues are not completely sealed off from the more practical decisions about what to do or say in actual encounters. Personal, private feelings will always have a tendency to leak into our behaviour in one form or another. Nevertheless, in substance they are rather different phenomena from those that concern our immediate behaviour and the responses we get from others. These issues are classically existential in that they relate to the inner private texture of our individual worlds. They represent an internal (and idiosyncratic) map of our social and psychological universe.

The map points to an array of possibilities for psychologically constructing our social and physical reality. They point to deep feelings and convictions that we hold about the world, our place in it, and our lived experiences of it. Moreover, these are existential questions about the way in which we perceive and experience ourselves, our bodies and our fundamental sense of reality. In a sense they constitute what might be thought of as our personal answers to the question What is the meaning of my life?

Existential alternatives		
Authentic (real) self	*v*	*Inauthentic (false) self*
Full aliveness	*v*	*Deadness in life*
Life as meaningful	*v*	*Emptiness, fear, anxiety*

With these deeper existential questions the emotions are more immediately and directly engaged because they are, in themselves, emotional by their very nature – concerning subjective feelings, moods, perceptions and thoughts. They concern responses to questions such as: In terms of what overall mood (pessimism, optimism, defeat or challenge) shall I live out my life? What kind of person shall I become? What will be my emotional outlook? How will I respond to the problems of life?

Real and false selves: the problem of being genuine

The question of the authenticity of the self revolves around the practical issue of how we feel about ourselves in a general sense. Do we feel real and authentic? For example, are our behaviour and actions sincere and genuine reflections of who we really are? Or do we have a nagging feeling that we are being false, putting on an act and covering over our real selves? A person who feels inauthentic in this sense may do so because they feel more comfortable about acting out a predetermined script rather than expressing their true selves.

They regard their true or real selves as unfit or unreliable for social purposes. Their authentic self is felt to be overly fragile and they see themselves as lightweight and insubstantial. Hence the true self is regarded as too vulnerable or too sensitive to survive the normal buffeting and bruising of routine social intercourse. By retreating behind a more socially acceptable facade attention is diverted from actual or imagined weaknesses around the self. In some cases this may even involve the adoption of a falsely aggressive or dominant posture to cover feelings of basic hurt or emotional inadequacy. Other cases may simply involve setting up barriers and practising non-disclosure. Erecting an emotional out-of-bounds has the effect of insulating the self from potentially undermining or discrediting attacks, insults or accusations. Of course, to some extent, we all incorporate elements of behaviour from a number of storylines or self-narratives that are relevant and acceptable within our cultural environment. In this sense, the self can never be completely unique. But this process becomes pathological when the individual retreats behind a set of stereotyped behaviours as a psychological defence.

Some people adopt false personas or perpetually hide behind an artificial performance for straightforwardly criminal or anti-social (deviant) purposes. For example, someone who commits fraud must present a false front in order to carry it through. Similarly paedophiles must create the illusion of safety and trustability in order to entrap children for sexual purposes. Also similar are serial killers who first get close to, and lure their target by pretending to be a normal regular guy (for example, Ted Bundy in the USA, Peter Sutcliffe in the UK).

At the other end of the scale of inauthenticity we have rampant egotists who attempt to deceive others into thinking that their power and importance in the world is far greater than it actually is. It could be argued that such individuals are engaged in a drama of deception about who they are. They could be said to be caught up in a world of total inauthenticity. Seemingly for them the dilemma between real and false selves has been resolved squarely on the side of artifice and illusion. But the key question is whether the individual is consciously aware of being inauthentic.

A criminal wielding a gun may be acting tougher than he really is, but at the same time he may identify with this image and convince himself that he actually is as tough as he's making out. An egotist will always exaggerate her or his importance and/or influence on other powerful or famous people, but actually believe that they do possess such extensive powers. And here the question of self-deception (rather than deception of others) comes to the fore. As long as you are in a state of self-deception (or 'bad faith' as Sartre (1966) puts it), you cannot apprehend or understand your inauthenticity.

The self and the problem of authenticity		
Authentic	*v*	*Inauthentic*
(Feeling real)	*v*	*(Feeling unreal)*
Self-knowledge	*v*	*Self-deception*
Good faith	*v*	*Bad faith*

Breaking through to authenticity

At some stage of their lives most people experience feelings of anxiety and discomfort about themselves and life in general. In one sense, blocking out such disturbing perceptions and thoughts is positively functional, it prevents a build-up of emotional pressure which could threaten to annihilate the self and destroy our credibility as individuals. However, the downside is that it also provides us with a set of blinkers and traps us in 'bad faith' or self-deception as Sartre puts it. As a result we are prevented from apprehending our true and natural state in the world. In this sense, being 'inauthentic' is being caught up in the conventional world and failing to question it, or even recognize it in the first place. It is to be unwittingly trapped in the world of conformity to social expectations, convention, rules, customs and traditions.

To be able to break through to authenticity demands a rigourous self-honesty, a willingness to be aware of our entrapment in conventional 'normality' and a decision to undergo the painful journey that breaking from it entails. The first step is to realize that one is living in a state of bad faith in the first place. This is made very difficult of course because of our tendency to deny or block out disturbing or threatening ideas. We are inclined to accept our own reasons and rationalizations for our beliefs and behaviour and tell ourselves stories we want to hear, rather than ones that are strictly true but inherently disturbing or disruptive.

Moreover, as Heidegger stresses in *Being and Time* (1962), the price to be paid for breaking through to awareness of (being in) this 'fallen' state is a chronic state of anxiety, a free-floating, objectless fear. This kind of anxiety is triggered by the awareness that our own existence is precarious and that self-extinction is a possibility. That is, we become aware of our potential nothingness (absence of self), and the nothingness that surrounds us. We realize our existential aloneness, that no one else can live our lives for us and that we (alone) are responsible for making what we can of ourselves (given that we are born with certain capacities and in particular circumstances). The apprehension of this nothingness may occur when we confront our own mortality and this is an alarm call which calls forth anxiety about the inherent insecurity of existence. This can also occur when we realize that we are ultimately free to decide who or what we shall become as an individual, as a person. Recognizing that this responsibility falls on our shoulders alone – no one else's – may precipitate an overwhelming feeling of uncertainty, confusion and insecurity. We come to see that social conventions are simply conveniences that we hide behind in order to protect and cushion us against our insecurity. Many common feelings such as the essential fragility of life, and our transience as 'mere' individuals in the context of human history, reflect some of our uncertainties and fears about death, and our concern to acquire some kind of significance in life. It is the fear that death will overtake us, or that we won't have time to do what we want to do in our lives that constantly reminds us of the fragility of human existence and the self.

To actually make contact with our authentic selves, we have to find a vantage outside and beyond the 'prison' of our own viewpoint. We have to see ourselves without the blinkers of preconceptions, assumptions and cherished beliefs about who we are. We have to penetrate through the many guises that our self-deceptions take, in order to see them as so many ways of convincing us that we do not need to develop or change. In fact, it takes a spirit of complete and critical openness about ourselves before we can embark on such a journey. However, given that the journey to self-understanding is such a difficult one, it is not surprising that many of us never embark on it, let alone complete it. Thus it is that so many of us remain trapped within what Heidegger terms the 'they self' (the socially defined, conventional self) while the 'homeless' authentic self stays forever beyond our reach. More often than not, those who do manage to set out to try to make contact with their deeper or real selves have to be content with an unsatisfactory compromise of imperfect self-knowledge. A sort of half-way house between authenticity and inauthenticity. This is, perhaps, the more realistic scenario. The pressing demands of modern life and the necessity to care about others as well as oneself, in all probability means that anxiety about self-authenticity can only be allayed on a situational, or case-to-case basis. Most probably, the attainment of the perfectly aligned 'true' self, has to be the exclusive preserve of those who have the time, resources and inclination to seek spiritual fulfilment on a full-time basis. But the rest of us should not conclude that our lifestyles and life-interests absolutely exclude the ideals and practical benefits (both for ourselves and others) of authenticity.

More important than the attainment of some perfect state of self-knowledge is active involvement in the *search* for authenticity and an appreciation of at least some of the practical issues that it raises. Being 'readily disposed' in this manner will ensure that we are more likely to engage with the ideals of authenticity at least some of the time. Acquiring a critical transformative attitude towards our habitual self-deceptions is an important beginning in this sense. Being able to see through our bigger self-deceptions is the only route to greater self-responsibility.

The self and aliveness

Do you really feel alive? Are you driven by enthusiasm and energy while tackling the daily chores? Do you feel joy and elation at simply being alive? Do you face life's problems in a positive and challenging way? Maybe you feel quite the opposite; that life is a drudge, that you have to drag yourself around doing things you'd rather not do. Do you lack energy, enthusiasm and enjoyment? Do you feel excluded from the core of life? Do you feel out of tune with life and that comunication is impossible? Do you feel only half alive, and unable to get in touch with the flow of life, the life force?

The self and the problem of aliveness		
Alienation (from self and others)	*v*	*Engagement, with life, involvement with others*
Being an observer (locked outside life)	*v*	*Being a participant (locked inside life)*
Ill-at-ease (out-of-touch)	*v*	*In touch with life (and self)*
More dead than alive (half alive)	*v*	*Fully alive (life-force energy)*
Detached self (unembodied)	*v*	*Embodied self (inside your skin)*

These are the stark alternatives associated with the existential question of aliveness. Most of the time you are more than likely to fall somewhere in between the two. Nevertheless, there are those who recognize, only too well, one or the other of the extremes as a way of describing the permanent quality of their lives. In particular, those who feel only half alive most of the time are very conscious of the general misery that comes with it. Of course, individuals vary in the extent to which they suffer in relation to these problems. Different people experience varying degrees of alienation both from themselves and others. They may feel more or less at home in the world or more or less detached from life.

The continuum between complete engagement and absorption in life, and complete alienation or estrangement from self and others is perhaps the main issue in relation to the aliveness of the self. But there are others which are often a part of the whole feeling syndrome. One of these is the experience of being an observer on the margins of life (as it passes you by). It is as if you were somehow locked on the outside and watching other people through a window, but you aren't able, or permitted to join in, for some reason which remains unclear to you. As an uninvited guest, all you can do is press your nose up to the window and peer in enviously, and wonder what it would be like if you could join in.

This separation from life or locked-outness, constrasts significantly with the experience of being a full participant at the dance of life, a fully accredited member of the human race. A person who engages with, and views life wholly from the inside, is typically committed, involved and enthusiastic about an array of interests. This complete absorption in immediate events (family and friendships, work and leisure time pursuits) automatically precludes the establishment of psychological distance from the process of living. These people are so fully immersed in, and gripped by, their experience of life that they're unable to contemplate it from the non-involved viewpoint of an observer.

Of course there are some individuals (perhaps the greatest number), who are an amalgam of these influences. This is why the idea of alien-ation or being an outsider or perpetual observer, are recognizable to most of us. There are times when we have fleetingly glimpsed what it might be like to be not included or univited to the party so to speak. In fact, it may well be that the primordial fear of being sidelined from life, is one reason why we have a natural tendency to flee (desperately, at times) from the possibility by immersing ourselves in activities and relationships. Such involvements automatically make us feel included, wanted (and loved of course), even if we are actually mistaken about this.

The problem of anxiety about nothingness, in the form of the annihila-tion of the self, is clearly related to this fear of non-inclusion or being an outsider. Being on the outside looking in is tantamount to the negation of the active side of the self (the self as the locus of agency). The sense of exclusion felt as a result of experiencing onself as an observer (rather than an active participant), directly threatens the core of the self – its capacity for efficacy, power, control and influence.

Being ill-at-ease and out-of-touch with self and others are also related to the experience of alienation and an outsider status. This implies not only a feeling syndrome – the moods and emotional accompaniments – of such a state of mind, but also the practical implications of the alienation experience. For example, it includes being out of touch with relevant social skills such as 'getting-on' with others, and attracting their com-pany, or having resources and capacities such as knowledge, know-how, charisma, personality and so on which would serve as attractors (see Chapter 4). Being in touch with your self involves what is generally referred to as self-knowledge – being able to judge your own emotional and practical limitations and potentials and being able to correctly identify and handle your own feelings towards people and events. It could be that the strongest image or metaphor capable of summarizing this group of feelings and experiences is that of 'deadness'. Although the present focus is on the issue of the relative aliveness of the self, it is perhaps even easier to envisage the emotional bleakness of this subjective state by viewing it in terms of degrees of deadness. Of course, we aren't literally talking about death (which means the complete absence of self), but we are speaking of death in life, sometimes referred to as a deadness of the soul. This raises an important question about awareness. It seems that those who experience a profound lack of enthusiasm, energy and general aliveness know what they're missing because they are continually focused on the void at the heart of their lived experience. By contrast, those who are fully vitalized by existence and are energized by the life force, are generally insulated from the flipside of life – blackness, bleakness and misery.

This suggests that those whose self-identities are anchored around negativity are likely to have a greater awareness of the depth of the experiential and emotional possibilities of life. In contrast, those who are eternal optimists, who always view life in positive terms and whose unhappiness is always superficial, temporary and fleeting, are more likely to be perceptually and cognitively limited by this view. What you don't see (or experience) you don't know. What you don't know you don't see (or experience). This is not a judgemental observation but merely one of fact – the perception follows the experience of greater emotional depth and the possibilities of life.

Those who feel barely alive and shut-out from important experiences in life, are also more liable to feel themselves lacking in significance and (hence) visibility, to others. In extreme cases such people may become so accustomed to being seen through or overlooked by others that they virtually acccept it as an immutable fact in their lives. Of course, being visible in this sense, is of central importance to the maintenance and generation of self-esteem, self-confidence and personal efficacy. And this is because being visible also means being recognized and valued as a person. It almost goes without saying that real evidence of significance (to others) gives support to a sense of genuiness, worthiness and self-respect.

The dislocated self

Laing (1969) famously spoke of the 'false' or 'disembodied self' in his analysis of the experience of schizophrenia and this concept has shed light on

117

the experiences of those suffering from serious mental illnesses. Here, I want here to draw attention to the rather more routine or everyday experiences and feeling states that involve the body and embodiment. I distinguish between what I shall call the 'dislocated' self and the 'embodied' or sitting self. The distinction focuses on a feeling of difference – between a sense of being 'inside your skin' as compared with feeling that your self-identity has become dislodged or displaced from inside your body – to some indefinite place. It denotes the difference between feeling at home in your body – in the sense of being relaxed and existing within its confines – and the feeling that you are in some sense estranged or alienated from yourself. You feel that your self is somewhere other than inside your body, but are unsure exactly where it resides. As a result, you feel that access to it is blocked and you are shut away from your self. This differs from Laing's ideas about the disembodied and embodied self in a number of ways.

Laing was concerned with serious mental disorder which also involves a breakdown in a person's sense of reality and a resulting lack of control over their lives and behaviour. The idea of the dislocated self does not imply a serious misperception of, or break with reality. Rather it points to a feeling (or mood) state which accompanies reflective consciousness. Such a state is indeed uncomfortable and even perhaps, anxiety-provoking because of the uncertainty produced by the dislocation of the self. But athough this may prove a drain on self-confidence and basic security, it does not normally hinder a person's ability to participate in social life or behave with propriety. Subjectively, however, they may perceive themselves to be incompetent and *feel* that their lives are out of control.

Related to this, Laing's distinction between the embodied (real) self and the disembodied (false) self pinpoints the problems faced by an individual who is fundamentally confused about who they are – perhaps literally believing they are someone else (even a historical figure reincarnated). The concept of the dislocated self does not imply such a serious confusion about identity. However, it does involve *some* (less obvious) confusion. For example, although their closest friends may not be really aware of it, the sufferer may habitually ask themselves questions such as: Who am I really? What was I sent here to accomplish? 'How shall I carry on? That is, subjectively the individual may feel confused about themselves and unsure about their abilities, although this uncertainty may not be obvious to others. In this respect it isn't something that massively interferes with their capacity to do their jobs properly, or to competently carry out normal duties responsibilities and expectations. Such uncertainty and confusion as there is operates behind the scenes as part of the private self which often remains undisclosed even to the closest and most intimate of associates.

In sum, self-dislocation creates chronic anxiety and uncertainty about the self which simply reinforces the problems associated with dislocation. The anxiety centres around a number of issues including the reliability of the self (its strength, confidence, security) as well as feelings of inadequacy and incompetence. The apparent absence and inaccessibility of the self may create uncertainty about its authenticity – the realness of personal identity. Combined, these effects weaken feelings of efficacy and agency and as a result the aliveness of the self is seriously diminished. The lack of alignment of body and self reflects an explicit denial and repression of emotions, needs, inclinations and yearnings that are normally expressed in the embodied self. Thus the other side of dislocation is full-embodiment.

In normal circumstances a healthy person experiences a relatively anxiety-free, relaxed and easy connection between body and self. This is an indication of general at homeness with themselves, their emotions, needs and desires. Of course, no one lives a completely trouble-free existence. By their very nature moods, emotions and feelings are volatile, dynamic and often unpredictable. However, psychological health depends upon the individual's at homeness in their bodies and minds.

The problem of meaning and existential aloneness

Problems of authenticity and aliveness tend to centre around inner self-reflectiveness (how you think and feel about yourself and how you get on, or fail to get on with other people as a result). In comparison, issues about the meaning of life itself, or the meaningfulness of our personal existence tend to be more concerned with our outward relation to the world and social environment.

Existential problems of meaning and emotion		
Existential aloneness	*v*	*Social connectedness*
		Spiritual connectedness
Meaninglessness	*v*	*Meaningfulness*
Nothingness (the void)	*v*	*Being and purpose*

In fact, the inner and outer dispositions of the self are connected in fairly complex ways. However, questions which focus on how meaningful our lives are, are never simply concerned with how much we know about life, or understand about our own predicament. As with all questions which bear upon the nature of the self, they intrinsically involve feelings, emotions and moods.

Problems of meaning and feeling responses		
Existential aloneness	:	*Self-responsibility, self-determination*
Meaninglessness	:	*Hopelessness, despair, anxiety, absurdity and arbitrariness (of life)*
Nothingness (the void)	:	*Fear, anxiety, dread, nausea*
Social or spiritual connectedness	:	*Togetherness, inclusion, oneness (with cosmos)*
Meaningfulness	:	*Hope, optimism, relaxedness contentment*
Being and purpose	:	*Love, inner peace, ego-suppression, embracement of the void*

Most of us tend to move between the extremes of feelings in response to problems of meaning but are generally somewhere in the middle. For weeks, months or even years, we might become shunted more to one side or the other as we encounter life's problems and respond either defeatedly or by resisting and overcoming them. But even within the daily round we are changeable creatures. We are inclined to see our day as a series of ups and downs, (good news and bad news) which are but small-scale versions of more dramatic examples. It is only those who are 'pathologically' optimistic or, those who have attained a level of spiritual transcendence who can reliably maintain a balanced and steady course through the troubles, problems, trials (even tragedies) of life.

Coming to the realization that we *are* existentially alone in the world can be a very disturbing experience. It is even more of a shock if we find, to our horror, that we have become (perhaps unwittingly) dependent on certain people or relationships. 'I couldn't live without...' is not an uncommon refrain in our self-talk or shared intimacies with those we love. It is also true that many individuals feel that once they lose a beloved partner their own life no longer has purpose or meaning.

It is frequently assumed that a belief in the fact of existential aloneness is completely antithetical to a corresponding belief in connectedness, interdependence, or spiritual union with others. However both beliefs have a certain validity. We are existentially alone in so far as we face death alone – no one else can die for us – and I presume few sane people would attempt to dispute this. But it is exactly the same with life. Ultimately, no one else can live our lives for us even if we wanted them to. It is, in the final analysis, only you yourself who can live out your life, experience your experiences, and make of yourself what you are capable of becoming. You may seek help from others. Others may, from time to time, take you under their wings and give you support practically, emotionally and materially. However, in the end it is only you who can benefit from the help, support and advice that others may provide. Only you can be a success or a failure in this respect. In short, as Sartre (1966) suggested, we are all free to make decisions about the kind of person we shall become. We are all personally responsible for the kind of person we are in any situation. Even under circumstances where we would seem to have no freedom or choice whatsoever, we are able to choose how we respond to those constraints. For example, in cases of extreme coercion (slavery, imprisonment and so on), although we may not be free to change the basis of our domination, we are free to select from a number of possible behavioural responses. We can respond with defiance and resistance, or with coolness and equanimity, or even acquiescently, as a helpless victim and so forth. Now as both Sartre and Heidegger suggested, the realization that we possess such levels of freedom and responsibility may create an almost intolerable degree of anxiety, uncertainty and confusion in those who have never either understood or considered it before.

However, it is also possible that those who do relish the idea of greater responsibilites may accept, or even embrace them, without fear or anxiety. In fact, achieving full authenticity is only possible by understanding and accepting the fact of existential aloneness. But this wouldn't necessarily be incompatible with a belief in the essential togetherness and connectedness of humankind. In this sense accepting aloneness has to be regarded as an essential basis on which to build more adequate and genuine bonds with others. That is, aloneness may actually subserve togetherness, and I shall examine this possibility further on.

There are those unfortunate souls who are so mired in the negativities and miseries of extreme loneliness (rather than aloneness), that they find the notion of aloneness a further threat to their already diminished self-esteem. They have come to view their own aloneness in unremittingly negative terms – as isolation and unhappiness. There are also those who do not find the notion of aloneness threatening to their self-esteem. In fact these people actually celebrate the importance of 'number one' because it supports their egos and self-esteem. For them, other people are primarily objects with whom they compete for status, scarce resources (consumer goods) or simple one-upmanship.

In this sense an exaggerated egotism is at odds with the co-operative and shared basis of good, healthy social relationships. Only where there is genuine reciprocity, and an equitable balance of giving and taking, do social relationships truly add to, and buttress the integration of the social community as a whole. Where a relationship or a social occasion is hijacked by the domineering behaviour of an egocentric individual, it has an erosive impact on social integration. Others begin to resent such ego-centric behaviour because it flatly ignores their own interests, feelings, and self-identities. As a result they try to resist or counter it by open con-frontation or stealth. Thus the integrative effects of positive bonds are lost and although the impact of a single instance on the wider social fabric may only be minor, it is nonetheless disruptive. However, an extensive grouping of such instances could do rather more serious damage to social integration.

Meaninglessness and meaningfulness

Although not frequently the explicit topic of conversation the question of whether life has meaning is often 'quietly present' or 'loitering with intent' around our most routine encounters with others. This may be because issues of meaning or lack of meaning are so closely associated with common feelings and emotions. Thus when life is meaningful for us we are charged with hope, optimism and contentment. The fact that our lives are meaningful to us is a sure sign that we are feeling happy, OK and in tune with life. And this is so even if, at the same time, our lives are peri-odically interrupted by what might be considered to be a normal quota of life's problems. Conversely, when we feel that life (or our life) is mean-ingless, we are usually without hope, often despairing and anxious. Sometimes when we really begin to question socially prescribed rituals and behaviour we become acutely aware of the absurdity of life, of its strange arbitrariness and its lack of solidity. As the existentialist thinkers have pointed out, we are 'thrown' into life without any say in the matter. We did not choose our parents or our circumstances, we were simply pre-sented with them when we were born.

Considered against this background there are times when we seriously ponder such questions as Why am I here? What is my purpose in life? Where is my life going? What is the point of life? Often there seem to be a distinct lack of sensible, meaningful answers to these questions, espe-cially when we reflect on them with some care. The beliefs and values that society holds sacred or important may suddenly appear alien or unre-lated to our own lives, problems and circumstances – the result of decisions made by distant others and about whom we know little. As a consequence, a lack of meaningfulness in our daily lives feeds into a lack of purpose and enthusiasm about life and activity in general.

What is the point of conforming to rules, values or social expectations if they are arbitrary? What is the point of doing anything if it is all a sham and without real purpose? In the face of such questions action is likely to 'bog-down' (Becker 1974). People who become seriously unhappy or mentally unwell (such as those suffering from depression) are susceptible to the emotional impress of this kind of meaninglessness. For them, the energy, purpose and motivation that usually makes us simply get on with life in an unquestioning manner is drained away and replaced by hopelessness, apathy, depair and anxiety. More typically, those of us who are not prone to great despair about the nature of existence, nor to pondering on the big questions of life are, nonetheless, often afflicted by associated problems of ennui, and lack of spontaneity and excitement that come with the dull habit and routines of daily life. These problems seem to arise where the original freshness of life has eventually been squeezed out of it through the constant re-enactment of domestic rituals and predictable work-day routines.

Even, constant contact with family, lovers, friends or colleagues may become empty of novelty and meaning. Our most familiar companions might not seem to offer the same degree of excitement and involvement that they once did. Both they (and us) have become yawningly predictable in our views, and behaviour. Even their supposedly off-the-cuff, humourous remarks seem to be retold variations along exceedingly familiar lines. Cohen and Taylor (1976) term this 'the nighmare of repetition' and document the many ways we attempt to escape the boredom and monotony of the routines, rituals and scripts which to a large extent give order to our daily lives.

By attempting to escape from the straightjacket of the demands of everyday life we are attempting to avoid the threat of meaninglessness. We desperately veer away from the emptiness and purposelessness which periodically threatens to take away *any* vestige of excitement, novelty and spontaneity from our social and personal experience. By being succesful in our escape attempts (say in the the form of hobbies, fantasies, games, gambling, drinking, drugs, sex, holidays), we manage to keep at bay the potentially distasterous effects of personal disintegration through the deadening effects of monotony, boredom and routine. However, a certain amount of routine may be potentially life-saving. A life of total chaos where nothing was predictable or reliable would indeed be another kind of nightmare. We need the comfort of some habits, rituals and routines to provide with us a minimal sense of security (Giddens 1991). Without such props on which we can hang some (not inconsiderable) part of our personal identities and in which we invest emotional energies, we would be bereft of a structural framework of support for the self. Such is the fineness of the line between so-called healthy 'adjustment' to life, and madness induced by repetition.

If routine is double-sided, so also are the consequences that the experience of meaninglessness can bring. For those whose lives are seriously impoverished by the experience, mental debilitation is the main and most crushing consequence. For those many others who feel acutely the chronic ennui of everyday ritual and routine the most tried and tested attempts at mental escape or psychological survival seem to suffice, at least in the short term (Taylor and Cohen 1976).

But there is another, more localized dimension of meaninglessness born out of a person's sense of frustration with their lives, work opportunities and neighbourhoods and the lack of stimulation and material and status rewards they offer. Boredom and monotony breed resentment and a search for excitement which takes those involved beyond the confines of conventional society. Thus it is that adolescent gangs, football hooligans, and 'badass' thugs, seek status and excitement through violence and crime. By transcending the mundane world and the normal standards of society they gain emotional and sensual satisfaction which cannot be otherwise obtained (Katz 1988). But just as important, and closely linked with this emotional enticement, is the lure of (deviant) 'status' which could drag them from obscurity and in so doing transform them from a nobody into a somebody to be taken into account.

This personal significance (and self-value) might include being known as a local hard man, or gang leader, or even by courting notoriety as the most evil or the most elusive killer who ever lived. Such star criminals may become famous, attaining almost celebrity status and sought after by newspapers, TV and film companies as subjects of public interest. Attaining significance and status in this way is part of the motivation for some criminals. They view it as a means of turning their social and psychological inadequacies and failures into noteworthy examples of transcendent evil.

Nothingness: friend or foe?

Without doubt a strong realization that there is a nothingness or emptiness at the very centre of existence can lead to a crippling of the power to act and the draining of life-force energy. The most common reaction is to try to suppress or avoid any such thoughts or feelings. But there is another way of adjusting to the void of nothingness which threatens the very security of our being. This view is informed by spiritual approaches to the question of being, particularly branches of Buddhism, in which the idea of nothingness or the void are seen merely as the end result of removing the illusions that stand in the way of our direct perception and understanding of reality. To travel back towards nothingness is no less than to penetrate beyond the facade of words, thoughts and sensations that cloud our minds and which prevent us from appreciating ultimate reality which is inexpressible in language and talk and cannot be grasped or owned by anyone (Watts 1962, Tolle 2001).

By stripping away the illusory veil of thoughts, feelings, sensations and preconceptions that we habitually impose on the world it is possible to finally achieve 'a peace which passeth all understanding'. This deliberately effortless and aimless journey both requires and enables us to stop striving to be something or someone else (a better, happier, person, to have more possessions, higher status and so on) and to appreciate and accept who we are now – in the present moment. Such a pathway also allows us to get in touch with our true (higher) selves by renouncing the petty and self-interested status strivings of the ego, and to be selflessly at the service of humanity.

Now while much of this is laudable and accords with a deep notion of the spiritually informed life, such a view also suffers from some of the same limitations as the self-help and self-transformation literature (which, unsuprisingly, often draws on Eastern philosophy). As I hope has been made clear throughout this book, the self is not simply a ego and neither is the ego exclusively self-oriented. But there are other Buddhist ideas about the emergence of a higher self which must be resisted. Much in the Buddhist pathway to the higher self is predicated on the elimination of desire and the tyranny of the senses which keep us bound to the 'wheel of suffering'. On this view human unhappiness, suffering, or pain in life is the result our persistent hankering for 'more' than we have (greater wealth, self-confidence, better health, good fortune and so forth). In this sense we are totally concentrated on a future state of affairs in which our desires will be fulfilled. This only has the effect of destroying our chances of happiness by displacing our concern with what we have in the present, with what we might have at some point in the future. However, when this point in the future has been reached we find that the original desire has simply been replaced by another. We are constantly robbed of fulfilment and satisfaction by being tied to a never-ending succession of sensuous desires which always remain out of reach in some unrealizable future.

There are two aspects which need to be questioned without in any way denying the well-intentioned character of this 'advice'. They concern the pursuit of sensuous desire and the tension and conflict between 'present' versus 'future' centredness. The advice that we should totally give up on desire and our chronic concern with its future fulfilment seems curiously out of kilter with both the demands of modern society and the needs of personal identity.

The idea that a future-orientation is a negative attribute because it takes us away from the now and binds us to an indeterminate future, does not square with the reality of everyday life and the demands it makes on us as individuals. Close examination of day-to-day life will reveal that it requires planning and foresight. No matter how much we may wish it otherwise, much of the organizational character of social life is based on a linear conception of time (from bus timetables to surgical operations, from air traffic control systems, to the celebration of birthdays and other calender-defined events). Thus, in order to function competently in such an environment we cannot afford to completely abandon a future orientation.

On more personal levels it would be impossible to mantain any sense of coherence in terms of self-identity unless we could imagine an unfolding future and project ourselves into it. Likewise, encounters will only go smoothly if we monitor and anticipate each other's responses and imaginatively 'rehearse' our own contributions (Mead 1967). So although it may be healthier mentally to try to cultivate a greater capacity for present-centred awareness and to be more appreciative of its value, it would be foolish simply to jettison any practical consciousness of the future. A more realistic approach would be to try and amalgamate these two modes of perception and awareness. Even if this proves difficult, it may be possible to come up with a formula which ensures that a periodic concentration on one mode would not simultaneously negate the value and effects of the other.

The idea of freeing ourselves from mental slavery and the wheel of suffering would seem, in principle, to be a good thing. If we are careful to distinguish between what we might call 'excess' desires and those which are essential to our continued healthy growth as individuals, then the injunction may indeed have some potential usefulness. Thus it would be to the advantage of all that exccessive appetites and desires for non-basic goods (and other more personalized desires) be moderated and modulated.

However, the question of desire in general is of a different order. The inner dynamics of self-identity are importantly about desire. The self is an organizing centre of desire-needs, and control strategies for their fulfilment. This is perhaps most obvious in the development of the human infant with its needs to receive love and support from its caretaker(s) in order to feel that it has become a central locus of positive value (Becker 1974). But this is equally true of the fully developed adult. Self-esteem needs and basic security needs remain essential throughout adulthood. This is true not only in the face of critical life problems, and existential dilemmas, but also in the day-to-day minutae of personal relationships and encounters. At the best of times a person's desire-needs are in a fragile state of balance.

If a person is under stress and/or trying to grapple with a serious life problem, this balance may already have been disturbed. Unless this imbalance is corrected the self will come under very severe pressure. Its whole existence may be threatened (as it certainly is in cases of serious mental illness). The idea that we should shrink back from desire in general in order to become our real, better, or higher selves seems contradictory. A denial or supression of core desire-needs can only eventuate at best in a husked or hollowed-out self. At worst it may signal the very death of the self.

Chapter Summary

- Periodically we have to come to terms with deep questions about the nature of our existence. Particularly difficult is the search for authenticity in relation to who we are and the kind of person we eventually become.
- Experiencing feelings of being more dead than alive can result from a lack of belonging and inclusion. Feeling visible (noticed) and having a sense of your own significance as a person are essential for generating self-confidence, efficacy and for avoiding self-dislocation.
- Problems of existential aloneness, personal responsibility and personal meaning are interlinked. We attempt to escape from the boredom of routine and ritual, but they are also necessary for ontological security.
- The experience of nothingness can be either positive (fulfilling) or negative (disturbing).

8

The Self as Emergent Narrative

Chapter Preview

- Self-identity is a continuously realized emergent narrative rather than a 'reflexive project' or 'revisable narrative'.
- The circuit of social and psychological influences that condition the process of self-realization, including the emotional and control motifs of the self.
- The social pathways of self-realization.

In this final chapter I draw together the most significant themes, issues and ideas about the self raised in this book. In so doing I want to outline a view of the self as a process of 'self-realization' which can otherwise be thought of as a continuously emergent narrative. To do this I shall develop and elaborate on the relatively simple model mentioned in Chapter 6. There, the self was understood as continuously created and recreated as a result both of the individual's own responses and the influence and impact of their life experiences, existential problems and so on. Thus the self continuously emerges from, and feeds back into the unfolding experiences of social existence.

```
                        Life experiences
Self ---------- Existential problems ---------- Emergent self
                        Dilemmas
```

To describe this process as clearly as possible it is also necessary to be unequivocal about what I mean by 'self-narrative'. Other authors have used the term rather differently and therefore it is important to clarify my own usage from theirs. More generally, a failure to acknowledge the distinction between the two meanings of self-narrative can lead to misleading claims about the nature of the self. I use self-narrative to refer to the actual unfolding storyline of the self (or psychobiography) as it emerges from a person's lived experience. Others have linked self-narratives or 'scripts' to the kind of stories we identify with, and tell ourselves (and other people) about our own lives.

In the latter sense, life stories or scripts are taken from cultural and social stocks of knowledge (films, stories, myths and so on), which then help to structure the way in which people live out their lives. Now while there is no doubt that we all identify with certain (mythic) ideas about ourselves and the direction and style in which we live out our lives, this must not be confused with the self-narrative as an actual emergent story-line. In short we must not confuse what we believe about ourselves, or what we would like to think about ourselves, with who or what we actually are, in the real circumstances of our lives.

To focus on how individuals think about themselves and their unfolding lives is to be in danger of always accepting an idealized and essentially fictive version of self-narrative. Such a view cedes far too much credence to an individual's capacity for (accurate) self-knowledge and underplays the human tendency towards self-deception and idealization. Also while it is true that we are *in part* responsible for constructing our own lives (our narrative storylines) it is not true that our volition and agency operate in the absence of social constraints imposed by the real circumstances of our lives and experiences.

Focusing on the self-narrative as an actual emergent process of self-realization corrects the rather naive tendency to accept at face value an individual's own stories about themselves. Thus individuals cannot change their self-identities at will any more than they can alter the circumstances of their lives at will. Agency and circumstance interact with each other to produce an emergent self-identity. This involves a confrontation between, on the one hand, the personality and emotional characteristics of the individual, and on the other, the exact social circumstances they are living through.

By formulating the process of self-identity formation and change in this manner, I am countering two assumptions about the modern self. These are first, that the self is simply 'a reflexive project' and second that it is a 'revisable narrative' (Giddens 1991). Both of these assertions contain only partial truths and as such they are also misleading. These assumed characteristics of the self assume far too much mastery and control – self-transformative capacities – to individuals. At best, ordinary people have only partial control over their experiences and life circumstances and these have a powerful influence on the formation of self-identity. There are many things which we are compelled to undergo irrespective of our wishes and attempts to avoid them.

A healthily formed self-identity is existentially anchored, stable and robust. This suggests the opposite of a revisable narrative which implies superficiality and flakiness. An open-endedly revisable narrative also implies a rather unhealthy self – weightless, continually recreating itself without reference to any wider social validation or anchoring. Such a view simply ignores the massively important influences of life events, problems and social circumstances such as illness, injuries, unemployment, poverty, death of partners, friends and family and how they effect identity formation.

I believe that the notion of a realization of self-identity through an emergent narrative expresses more adequately the experience of the modern self. Although humans are active, inquiring and creative, they are also 'undergoing' beings as well (Becker 1974). There is a dialectic between whatever agency the self possesses and the social circumstances which influence and shape its trajectory through the social world. The actual extent to which the self-narrative is revisable is always limited, conditioned and constrained by external circumstances. It is never simply a reflexive project at the behest of the desires and transformative powers of the individual.

Self-realization

Although it might seem to have a lot in common with the term self-actualization, self-realization actually has a rather different emphasis and connotation. To some extent the term self-actualization has seeped into general usage but was originally brought to prominence in the work of the 'humanistic' psychologists Carl Rogers and Abraham Maslow. Maslow in particular, thought of self-actualization as a drive to fulfil one's potential as a human being and that its achievement is the highest point in a person's growth or self-development. Maslow argued that given that we each have various talents, skills and capacities they should be developed to their optimum point so that we can actualize our potential and put it to good use. In this sense self-actualization means the attainment of optimum mental health, wholeness and fufilment. It also includes a special awareness of the world, including a greater appreciation of beauty and undergoing what Maslow refers to as 'peak-experiences', and so on.

Unlike self-actualization self-realization is not about attaining one's long-term potential as such, but is about the *realization* of the self in the immediacy of everyday life and social interaction. It doesn't require or involve any special skills, capacities or experiences (as in peak-experiences). Self-realization is not a momentary, extraordinary, or transcendental experience; it is a continuous process firmly embedded in social practices and the mundane details of human behaviour. Also, self-actualization is concerned mainly with higher forms of behaviour, that which are essentially good, principled and ethically correct. Self-realization, however, refers to a process through which the self-identity of an individual evolves regardless of whether this self is good or bad, a higher self or a criminal self. It refers to the way a particular self unfolds or emerges in response to a unique configuration of life experiences, and existential problems. However, self-realization does require a person to make moral choices about the kind of self he or she will become in the light of the conditions that are given and which either help or hinder them in the process.

Self-realization also differs from Carl Jung's concept of 'individuation' which refers to a search for integration and wholeness of personality and also has a spiritual side to it. Jung was of the view that it was only in later life, after the success goals of power, status, sexual love and so on, had either been achieved, or had lost their hold or enchantment that individuation may take place. Only then may a person become detached from mundane emotional entanglements and ego-driven goals and become concerned with 'higher' pursuits and questions such as the meaning of existence, personal identity and self-fulfilment. With this view individuation is confined to a small period in an individual's life (as well as a restricted group of successful people) and carefully sequestered from more mundane preoccupations. In contrast, self-realization has a much wider application. First, it is a process in which the individuation of self-identity occurs continuously throughout a person's lifetime. That is, a person's individuality, their unique personal identity is continuously being shaped and reshaped. People are chronically concerned and involved with the question of who they are, and who they would like to be. There is no point at which this process starts or stops. It may become a more or less pronounced at certain times but it never ceases. Second, as a pragmatic process, self-realization is not neatly separated from the higher or more spiritual concerns of life but is neutral with regard to them. The self-realization of a specific person may or may not involve higher spiritual elements.

Figure 8.1 expresses the circuit of influences on the self which contribute to the process of self-realization and the emergent narrative of the self over time. It also indicates the sequence of the following discussion about the nature of, and connections between, the elements that go to make up the circuit of influences. Thus I begin with the nature of the self and its emotional security system and then move on to the psychobiography of the self and its relationship with the individual's current life situation. The latter is a crucial component in the circuit of influences since it functions as the mediating link between the individual self and the

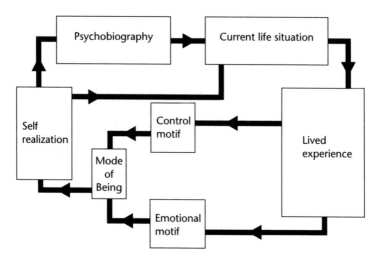

Figure 8.1 Circuit of influences

conditioning influence of his or her social circumstances. It also provides the bridge between life experiences and problems as they influence the development of the control and emotional motifs of the self. Finally, the combined effects of control strategies and emotional need dispositions combine to form six general pathways of self-realization. But the process is a continuous one. As it completes its first cycle (of realization) the self is already into the next – passing through further phases of current life situation and existential problems, and so on. As with all the elements in the process, the self evolves and reshapes itself as it accommodates the conditioning impress of these elements. But the extent and pace of change can never be specified in general terms. These depend on the specific individual and their exact social circumstances.

The nature of the self

I began this book by suggesting that personal identity is best understood in terms of: its social and psychological nature; the emotional basis of motivational needs; its reflexivity and flexibility; its executive capacity in terms of self-efficacy, competence and control; and finally, its potentially spiritual nature. I also suggested that the internal structure of the self is characterized by several levels of awareness and ego-functioning.

These characteristics furnish us with a picture of the operational self that in part forms a unifying centre of awareness (Branden 1985). Such a view certainly accounts for the reflexive awareness of the self. Additionally, given that forms of sub-consciousness and primary awareness play a part in the constitution of the self, this view may also embrace some part of the emotionality of the self. But on its own the idea of the self as a unifying and organizing centre of awareness implies a rather passive, information-processing image of the self, something that it most definitely is not.

The self is, par excellence, an executive centre. It is not solely an organizing locus of sensory input that operates as a collection and storage point for awareness and information absorbed from the environment. It is the primary centre of (self) efficacy, competence and personal control (over self and others). In fact the self is an activation and distribution mechanism-with-feelings! As such it mobilizes whatever resources are available to it, to cater for its own and other's needs, intentions and purposes. It is important to acknowledge that as individuals we do not stand alone, we are intermeshed with others in a network of social ties, defined by the person's current life situation.

Now the fact that in some individuals these executive functions have become subdued, dampened down, or almost completely suppressed, actually underlines their importance in the first place. For if they are functioning less than optimally a person's inner powers to transform, or make changes to their life circumstances will be handicapped to a commensurate extent. What is a stake here is the very capacity to act, per se. To the extent that the internal core of the self has been damaged then this executive capacity itself will be undermined, and as a result, so will its ability to translate whatever powers it possesses into practical action.

But the executive capacities for control, efficacy and competence must not be seen in limited terms as a set of purely cognitive operations. Central to an understanding of the self is its emotionality and this is no less important in providing an underpinning foundation for the self as an executive agent in the world. The efficiency and viability of the executive capacity of the self is closely related to the presence (or absence) of a central core of basic security which provides a foundation for the individual's self-esteem and confidence. As Becker (1974) has described it, this requires the self to be a solid and dependable 'positive locus of self-value'.

Basic security and psychobiography

Many writers have observed that early experiences with caretakers are of pivotal importance in the establishment of a child's basic sense of security in the world. A warm and loving environment in which the child is encouraged to explore the world and develop her capacity to manipulate various aspects of the environment would certainly be conducive to the creation of such basic security. Almost as crucially those same conditions would also nurture the development of a protective shield against potential threats to the self. A protective layer of basic security provides the child with some insurance against failure as it makes more extensive explorations in the world and searches for autonomy and the elaboration of its individuality.

That said, the idea that such early acquired basic security will prove to be a permanent guarantee against failure or vulnerability should not be countenanced. Neither should the converse idea that those who do not receive their early 'dose' of basic (ontological) security will inevitably be troubled by it and suffer emotionally and psychologically. A basic security system does not operate like this. By its nature it is a delicate and fragile balance of forces, thus it is not permanently able and ready to repel all manner of threats. But neither is a badly nurtured and weak security system destined to remain so irrespective of a person's subsequent experiences.

Security is not something you can own or possess once and for all. It needs to be constantly worked at, tended and cared for, in order for it to maintain good health. Life events such as the death of a loved one can seriously damage the defences of someone who is generally thought to be 'invulnerable' with a robust foundation of confidence and self-esteem. Similarly, acquiring a new skill such as public speaking may become a source of confidence and emotional protection in a person who previously has been nervous, anxious or phobic about social situations. In this sense, life events themselves can undermine, reinforce, or create anew various aspects of basic security. But basic security systems are prone to vulnerability in even more immediate ways. Situations or events themselves may be graded in terms of their 'demandingness' with regard to the protection of security (confidence, self-value, self-esteem). Obviously, speaking in public, in general terms, is more challenging as far as feeling secure or insecure is concerned, than say, sitting in your kitchen chatting with your partner. Although of course, how the situation plays out will determine exactly how trying or otherwise it actually proves to be. For instance, to your astonishment your partner may suddenly announce that the relationship is over and that he or she is leaving immediately!

Even in the smallest and most fleeting of meetings or encounters someone may make a remark that stuns you to the quick and leaves you momentarily at least, unhinged and humiliated. For some individuals one insensitive comment (deliberate or accidental) correctly aimed has enough penetrative power to rip through their protective armoury. For others, this may simply result in a rather embarrassing and clumsy up-ending, itself fleeting, quickly forgotten and with social poise restored (like a strong effective football tackle from which both players emerge relatively unscathed). However, it is also possible that the damage may linger and fester adding to the possibility of long-term injury to the person's emotional and psychological well-being.

In all these ways, basic security can never be guaranteed or taken for granted. It has to be constantly earned, negotiated and fought for, in the uncertain and often confusing environment of social interaction. The idea that the child receives an original, optimum amount of ontological security from his or her caretakers which remains naturally charged and maximally protective is erroneous. So is the idea that a less than optimum amount generated in childhood cannot be compensated for as life proceeds and personality develops. Although the child most certainly receives a fixed quota from his or her caretakers this is not fixed forever. As I've pointed out this depends on numerous other in situ and developmental factors.

Current life situation

The term 'current life situation' might seem simple enough in a common sense rendering of it, but crucial aspects are lost in a common sense interpretation. Most importantly, current life situation may seem to suggest something static, frozen or fixed in time. But these qualities are the very opposite of those I wish to convey by the term. In fact current life situation is part of an ongoing process which underpins the emerging narrative of the self (and bearing in mind the distinction between the two meanings of self-narrative made at the begining of the chapter). Two aspects need some elaboration. First, it is important to distinguish between current and biographical life situation even though they run into each other in practice. However, to see them only as all of a piece obscures the fact that in an important way we live out our lives from the vantage point of the present. Certainly, what we have or have not done in the past will have influenced who we have become. Thus the imprint of this past will press into the present as we head towards an (anticipated) future that stretches out before us and will, in time, also affect our sense of who we are. However, we must not overlook the fact that our current and immediate situation plays a large part as a point of origin for our actions. Our current nexus of social relationships (and the social encounters they involve), is importantly different from those past networks – even though some elements of the past may survive in the current situation and on into the future.

The future though is something of an open book, a distant and indeterminate horizon. We may anticipate which relationships and what circumstances will continue to play, or will come to play a significant role in our lives, but we can never know enough in advance to predict this accurately. The past and future, then, are compressed into the immediacy of the unfolding present. Existentially we are locked into the present and through thought and action we push towards a relatively unknown social future (although, of course, we may be only too aware that death is our ultimate destination).

It is only those relationships and people with whom we are currently involved and those events and circumstances that we currently face in our lives, that we can look to, to inform our decisions and behaviour. We anticipate and project the idea that this current configuration of people and circumstances will influence our destinies and it is within this context that we must work towards our future. The past, then, comes to play an important but indirect role in a person's current life situation. It is what the past, in terms of experiences, relationships, significant events existential conflicts, and so on, *has come to,* in the current situation, that in an important sense determines our view and orientation to the future.

Emotional tenor (or feeling tone) of current life situation

Current life situation then is the summation of a person's relationships and social involvements – what they have come to, expressed as an extant network of ties and interdependencies. Such a network is an evolutionary emergent from an individual's life history and biographical trajectory. Clearly, such a concept must make reference to a person's present social and material conditions of life such as their class, gender, social status and income circumstances, lifestyle, consumption patterns and so on, as well as how all these variables are embedded in the social network. However, such material elements simply provide the backdrop to a more important dimension of the network which I refer to as the 'emotional tenor' or 'feeling tone' of the current life situation. Thus, it is the psychological predisposition of the 'focal' person at the centre of the network that is the point of interest. Their state of mind, their projected vision as they contemplate the meaning of their overall situation, expresses and reflects the emotional impact of what has, or hasn't happened in their lives. It reflects the extent to which their private and personal expectations, hopes and wishes have been thwarted or fulfilled.

Crucially, the nature of the feeling tone that surrounds and envelops the person (frustration, satisfaction, despair and so forth) feeds directly into their sense of self-identity. This is because it raises questions about the sustainability and viability of the person's current self-narrative (script or life-plan) in the emergent circumstances of her or his life. These are questions about whether the self and its narrative line (or trajectory) are appropriate in current circumstances.

The emotional tenor of the situation provides an indication of how the person has dealt with life's problems and existential dilemmas (of both a deep and more superficial kind). It is a juncture at which the person reflects on what the future is likely to hold, whether he or she can meet its challenges and the kinds of psychological adjustments (radical or minor), that may be required. It is a key to the direction or pathway that the self will take in terms of its future development.

Current life situation, lifestyles, and self-narratives

Unlike many concepts about social life such as status, friendship, or consumer groups, a person's current life situation is not something he or she shares with anybody else. In this respect it also different from the idea of a 'social script' (Cohen and Taylor 1976) as well as the notion of 'lifestyle' which, Giddens (1991) argues is a defining feature of modern society and an important link in creating the narrative of self-identity. However, current life situation is not a socially shared experience such as dressing in a certain style, or in designer labels, choosing friends from certain cliques, or participating in particular leisure pursuits.

A person's current life situation cannot be understood as a collectively shared activity or pursuit in which they choose to participate. It has to be seen from the focal individual's point of view as a network of ties and interdependencies in which they are embedded and is unique to them. This unique configuration of relationships, commitments and experiences with its own distinctive feeling tone is completely individualized in the sense that it is pertinent to only one person. Even people close to this person, such as friends or family, will not share exactly the same network – there will always be differences in personnel, circumstances and above all, differences of a personal and psychological kind based on experiential and emotional factors.

I'm not suggesting by any means that concepts referring to socially shared activity are without relevance. However, they cannot replace the idea of a unique, emerging self-narrative which is significantly influenced by a person's current life situation. The concepts of lifestyle and social scripts, in particular, seem to be ill-suited to describing or explaining the radically individualized character of the emergent self-narrative. In this respect, the self-narrative, as it is conditioned by the current life situation is not ready-made as are lifestyles and scripts. It is not something already available that we can adopt or incorporate into our behaviour. It isn't like an article of clothing that we can take off a hook and try on for size, or choose to wear at appropriate times. While we are to a large extent in control of the creation of our self-identities, there are many things which simply happen to us and over which we have little control. We may be able to choose how we respond to what happens in our social world, but we cannot always influence what happens in the first place.

For instance, we cannot usually control or influence the lives of other people with whom we have ties and on whom we depend in various respects. A partner, friend or relative may die and leave us emotionally devastated. A business partner or employer may suffer catastrophic economic failure. Such events will impinge on our current life situation regardless of our wishes, and our ability to do anything which could prevent them happening. In this sense the unfolding narrative of the self cannot be abandoned or adopted like a lifestyle or a script, it is something that we have to live with and live through. In the process the self is in a constant state of emergence.

Characterized in this manner the self-narrative which, in experiential terms, constantly emanates from a person's current life situation, denotes the reality of what happens to us and how we personally respond. It sensitively registers an individual's real engagement with the world, the life problems encountered, the existential dilemmas endured. We have to work our way through these engagements, dilemmas, problems and commitments accepting what we cannot change and constructing our personalized responses to the events and circumstances in which we find ourselves. In this sense the self is the centrepoint of the unfolding story.

Without doubt we can, in the process, draw upon established scripts and lifestyles, as models and resources and social archetypes which may act as creative guidelines for a potential self-narrative. However, in the final analysis these can only be guidelines, or starting points for the creation of the self-narrative. It is only possible for the realized or actual self-narrative of an individual to emerge from the ongoing dynamic of influences as they are conditioned by the current life situation.

Critical events and life problems

Critical events and life problems are part of the emerging circumstances that a person must grapple with in attempting to fashion a self-identity. Generally they reflect the lived experiences of the individual as they happen, including critical events or life-changing incidents. By definition such events and incidents are non-routine and often unpredictable. Hence they have an immediate impact on the psychic reserves and morale of the individual. Clear examples of critical, life-changing events are the sudden onset of life-threatening (or terminal illnesses) or injuries that are physically disabling. Although apparently infrequent, they could happen to anyone at anytime. They require substantial modifications of self-identity to enable the person to adjust to the changed circumstances. Very important in this regard is a person's ability to come to terms with the reduced capacities and skills that attend such illnesses and injuries. Given the huge psychological and emotional impact of such events, someone who has self-esteem, pride and self-value invested in their physical fitness and self-sufficiency will be presented with what might seem almost insuperable difficulties of readjustment. Similarly, the death of a loved one may pose equally difficult problems of readjustment. However, profound identity changes may result from very positive experiences as well. Getting married, becoming a parent (or grandparent), being promoted, being recognized by the community, winning money, winning an election, recovering from illness, falling in love, learning a new skill, taking up a new hobby are all life-changing events that have significant implications for identity.

However, both negative and positive life events do not always have long-term identity consequences. A promotion may lead a person to feel that they have too much responsibility and that they were happier and less stressed in their previous position. Newly weds may find that the heady early days of marital bliss all too quickly decline into spats, tensions and even, estrangement. The exact circumstances in each (individual's) case will be decisive for self-identity. This simply underlines the importance of the individual's current life situation on the emerging self-narrative.

Sudden, unexpected events immediately put into question the viability of the current view of self. But other life problems are more gradual and accretive. Relationship problems are typically of this nature and often result from poor communication between the partners (be they lovers or just good friends). When both partners are not communicating properly there is a build up of unresolved (identity-related) problems such as feeling unwanted or un-listened to, or over-controlled. The emotional intensity in such a relationship may grow to explosive proportions and have damaging consequences for the relationship and the personal identities of both partners.

But relationships don't necessarily have to be problematic in order to initiate identity change. Partners may drift apart without any critical incident, overt trauma or disagreement. Sometimes partners simply change and develop over the years, becoming strangers to each other without even realizing it. On the other hand, as the years pass, partners may become more committed as they find more and more in common with each other. As the self-narrative unravels in this manner, personal identity undergoes gradual and orderly change.

Emotional motifs of the self

Earlier I suggested that a useful way of understanding the important existential dilemmas of life is to see them as variants of the basic tension between separateness and relatedness (or independence and involvement). This perspective also throws light on the broad spectrum of emotional motifs potentially available for self-adoption. Given that the basic dilemma of action is a result of the working tension between the dual forces of subjective and social reality, it is possible to understand the extremes of mental health and mental disorder or disturbance as a further reflection of this tension.

If we accept – and it is surely hard to disagree – that mental disorder represents a form of alienation or estrangement from social life and social relationships, then mental health represents a person's integration with social life and hence their involvement or social relatedness. This simply reaffirms the importance of good social connectedness for a person's mental health. In short, the more the individual becomes self-absorbed and removed from the bondedness of social relationships then the more likely is she or he to experience mental ill-health.

In Chapter 2 I sketched a model of a healthily functioning self based on the assumption that it requires the fulfilment of basic security and self-esteem needs. These include self-approval, love, respect, acceptance, confidence, self-worth, feelings of significance, recognition, a normal desire for aloneness (personal space), as well as togetherness and belongingness, feeling believed in, and properly understood. These are self-needs in the sense that the individual must experience themselves in these terms in order to function in a healthy manner. But, it is equally important that the self is able to elicit these responses from other people – that is to be loved, to be approved of, to accepted, and so on – in order that a proper balance of mental forces can be achieved. There must be a symmetry between self-feeling and the feeling responses received from others in order that they mutually support each other within the individual's psyche. This, in turn, is an essential requirement for attaining balanced interdependent relationships between people. If, for example, a person loves another but does not love herself, this will create a pathology in the bond, an over-dependence or a co-dependence rather than a healthily balanced mutuality.

In the light of these requirements then, mental health itself may be characterized by feeling authentic or real and having a firm sense of identity; feeling deserving of love and happiness and being animated by an aliveness and in touch with life energy. Mentally healthy individuals feel appropriate to life, that they are competent and efficacious, and sure that they are able to meet the challenges of life in a productive and effective manner. As such they will generally operate from a loving (caring, empathetic) attitude and be able to trust and have confidence in others. This characterization is, of course, an ideal in that most people will, perhaps at different times, frequently fall short of these indicators of mental health. The average person will, therefore, operate within a normal range of deviation from this standard, but will not fall below a level which marks the boundary between mental health and ill-health. Following through the logic of this characterization (but bearing in mind its idealized and hence exaggerated, nature) we can depict mental ill-health in the following manner.

An individual with poor mental health is likely to feel that they are living a lie in so far as they detect a falseness or phoniness about themselves. Sartre's idea of 'living in bad faith' or being shrouded in self-deception would seem an appropriate evocation of this state of mind. Poor mental health would also engender a conviction of non-entitlement to, or undeservingness of the rewards and fruits of life, particularly the right to love and happiness, as would feelings of deadness or exclusion from life. An alienation from the vibrancy of life and life-force energy would parallel a feeling of wrongness for, or inappropriateness to life.

A lack of basic security and self-esteem needs would provide a very fragile basis for identity which, as a result, might collapse, dissociate or fragment. The individual whose experience of themselves and others is like this would be chronically anxious. That is, both in company and alone, her or his reactions would be fear based, anxiety-ridden and non-trusting; relations with others would often be conflictual, tense and difficult. The person's insecurity might be directed outwardly at others and expressed as anger, blame, suspicion and resentment. More than likely, this would engender avoidant responses in other people, further intensifying fear of, and estrangement from others.

Alternatively, the response to insecurity could be inner-directed, producing self-blame, anger and self-punishment. It might register itself socially by a tendency to avoid contact, and an inability to sustain friendships and other forms of intimacy. Again, the responses are fear-based, but directed inwardly rather than towards others. In this case, a breakdown or collapse in agency will result in a general inability to act efficaciously, feelings of helplessness, hopelessness and of not being able to cope. Overwhelmed by circumstances, the person will feel that they are rapidly losing control of themselves and their lives.

Because of basic insecurity and a deficit of self-esteem, both the inner and outer-directed types would suffer serious confusions around identity. This would be exacerbated (and to some extent caused) by the chaotic and disorderly nature of their lives. A lack of control over self and the current life situation are common to both inner and outer-directed types. The significant difference lies in the mode of response to the control crisis. The outer directed type would perceive the external environment as the cause of the problem thus punishments directed at others and the world in general would be favoured over self-blame. If these characteristics represent the extreme of unhappiness and unhealthy mental functioning, then we now have some idea of the wide spectrum of self-feeling that lies between a healthy and unhealthy mental life, between vibrant happiness and chronic misery. Of course, the two extremes I've described are generalizations as well as exaggerations and as such, must not be (mis)taken as descriptions of actual individuals. They are general groupings of symptoms and self-characteristics. Particular individuals will possess varying amounts of these, but they will occur in unique combinations depending on their personalities, upbringing, and experience of life events.

Bearing in mind the generalized character of these descriptions, let us turn to the middle group of possible emotional self-motifs. This group, which is by far the largest of the three, reflects more than any other the average everyday individual. Such people experience an overall balance in their emotional lives. They tend to experience both highs and lows but generally don't stray out of a socially acceptable range and intensity of emotional expression and behaviour. Typically the individual is, at different times, as likely to experience depression as elation and joy depending on the context and situation.

This covers a wide range of variation in the personalities of particular individuals. Some, of course, will tend to exhibit stereotypical behaviour such as the person who always seems to be hopefully optimistic and enthusiastic, or another who generally surveys the world negatively and isn't interested in anything outside a narrow range. However, such variation in demeanour and motivation all fit within a normal range of acceptability. No one in this group is permanently confined in a straightjacket of inappropriate emotions and behaviours. They are not, for example, permanently locked into negative moods and emotions such as frustration, anger or despair. This group reflects the range of variability (of feeling, and behavioural demeanour) displayed by average individuals. For example, someone who becomes depressed over the loss of a loved one, but who after a period of bereavement returns to their normal buoyant self, or someone who is initially elated at finding their soulmate but who is later crushed by finding that they have several other lovers.

Many people are able to move rapidly between different feeling tones and intensities. It is possible to experience anger and frustration with the journey to work, but having reached it, to become overjoyed at the news that you or your department has won a particular contract (commission, tender or submission). Finally, on returning home you are plunged into depression (and anger) because the builder has left your house in a complete mess!

Self-realization and control motifs

If we follow the direction of flow of influences on the emergent self in Figure 8.1 (p. 132), it is clear that there is an interfusion of influences between psychobiography, current life situation, ongoing existential dilemmas, life problems and emergent critical events. These influences combine to fashion an individual self stamped by a specific emotional-cognitive motif – a way of confronting or engaging with the world on a basis of feeling. But this happens only in conjunction with the acquisition of a control motif for the self. In this sense, the emotional-cognitive and agency-control aspects of the self are welded together in a composite unity. There can be no feeling tone to the self without a corresponding control motif: they subserve each other and are indivisible.

What are the control motifs of the self? In Chapter 4 I identified three different types of control (benign, stolen and exploitative) and four typical strategies associated with the benign type. An average, healthily functioning social life will, in the main, be based around mutual benign control. But an individual's life overall might include a mixture of overlapping styles. There are usually some areas of life, or specific relationships in which the person doesn't have the upper hand. For example, it is often the case that those who hold authority or status in the public sphere appear to be dominant and manipulative in their relationships. However, when it comes to more private, intimate or domestic spheres some control relations may be reversed. Such individuals may be under the thumb in relationships with close family members or partners and forced to adopt defensive or indirect strategies of control.

For each person there will be a different and unique spread of relationships and areas in which control can be exerted (a feature of the current life situation). Again an average, normal, healthy life situation will be one in which there is a balancing-out of control in terms of each relationship and the overall nexus of relationships. Healthy forms of control are those which are balanced and effective and in which mutual benign control predominates. The spread of control in the life situation becomes unhealthy when exploitative or stolen styles of control outnumber other styles.

Within a single relationship, of course, we can speak of a healthy balance of control, or an unhealthy slide into too much control (dominance) or too little control (subjection). In much the same vein, we can understand the nature of the balance and style of control between an individual and his or her network of social ties as an indicator of normality or pathology. The key combination of influences in the process of self-realization is between the individual's emotional and control motifs. This amalgamation forms a provisional self which must engage with the individual's current life situation before it can take executive action and undergo the circuit of influences. Of course, a wounded and thus weakened self would interact with the current life situation in rather more defensive ways, possibly in a resigned or defeatist manner. Nonetheless it is the collision between the experienced self (composed of emotional and control motifs) and a particular kind of life situation that generates the emergent process of self-realization.

Social pathways of self-realization

It is not possible to capture the unique individuality of the self that emerges from the process of self-realization, without following the trajectories of particular individuals – and that is beyond the confines of this study. However, as a preparatory step in this direction it is possible to speculate about the more general parameters within which this uniqueness is formed. Thus by taking into account some possible combinations of the variables already discussed as essential to the general process of self-realization, we can also discern some possible, generalized pathways towards self-realization.

The combined effects of emotion, control and current life situation produce an emergent self-identity which is then channelled via the individual's ongoing life situation into one of several socially recognizable pathways. The cycle of influences is repeated, leading either to a reconfirmation of the self or to minor or major changes (modifications and adjustments) in the self while remaining within the parameters of the existing pathway. However life-changing events or problems may precipitate

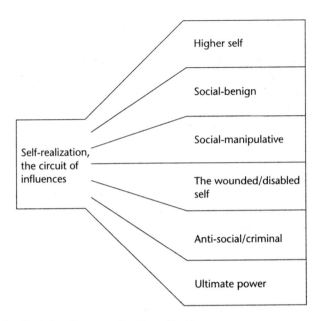

Figure 8.2   Social pathways of self-realization

a switch in a pathway with consequent major alterations in identity and self-narrative.

I distinguish between six social pathways of self-realization (Figure 8.2). These are not meant to be exhaustive or definitive and it is also clear that there could be further sub-divisions within the pathways as well as over-laps between them. However, my intention is to highlight the general links between the concepts and variables that comprise what I've termed the circuit of influences on the emergent self-narrative. I also want to illustrate the effects of these influences as they result in particular out-comes for the self, as well as the wider society. I'll deal with them in the order they appear in Figure 8.2.

The higher pathway

The higher pathway, of course, is that of the higher self as I've described it at several points in the book. Nurturing the higher self involves a delib-erate development of the self away from an entrapment in egotistic self-ishness and narcissism, towards a much more altruistic attitude and orientation. This may be achieved by private study of spiritual or religious texts or by becoming a believer or adherent of some faith or set of spiritual principles or practices. In either case a genuine and/or full-time involvement or adherence is required to achieve a certain level of consciousness, as is a certain distance or emotional disengagement from the mundane world. Because of the required level of detachment from worldly pursuits, it can be appreciated that full or proper engagement with this pathway is barred to large numbers of people. The majority of people in the modern world are dependent on an income from mainstream economic activity and would find such alternative, or additional commitments impossible.

For those few who are committed full time to a spiritual or religious pathway to the higher self, the ultimate goal is to reach a balanced state of mindfulness. In practice this means a mental equanimity derived from a rejection of, and detachment from, worldy desire, ego-striving, achievement, competitive individualism, and the domination or exploitation of others. Instead, the individual adopts a non-materialist creed based on kindness to others, generosity (both material and emotional), egalitarianism and non-violence. The creed also endorses the view that the highest way of being is based on the recognition of the oneness of humanity as a whole and disparages feelings of individual separateness or specialness.

These assumptions are founded on the belief that the experience of (egotistic) separateness derives from a societal focus on individuality, status and power differences, and an emphasis on personal achievement and gratification (deferred or immediate). The objective of the higher path, therefore, is to transcend such worldy attachments in order to achieve spiritual connectedness with the rest of human kind. In this sense much of what Maslow says about self-actualization and peak experiences, and what Jung refers to as the process of individuaton as a search for greater self-knowledge and personal integration, are in line with these values and objectives. However, most of those who are favourably disposed to the ideas, principles and values around the higher self and who are willing to at least partly relinquish the status and material rewards and satisfactions of capitalist consumerist society are only able to pursue the pathway on something less than a full-time basis. In this sense this stratum of the higher pathway overlaps with the one immediately below it – the social-benign path. This is also the point at which there is a marked convergence between altruistic values (care and compassion for others) based on purely spiritual and religious sources and those based on a morality derived from the social order of interaction and interpersonal relations. What these segments have in common is the notion of a self-identity and social existence founded on an overwhelming belief in the use of benign control (or influence as such individuals would no doubt prefer to call it), in interpersonal matters.

The social-benign pathway

Since there has already been a distinction drawn between the full-time and part-time commitment to an engagement with the route to the higher self, it is no real surprise that this one also benefits from sub-division. The upper section shares much in common with the one above it in terms of an altruistic morality of care and compassion for others and the use of benign control. However, in this case the interpersonal ethics of mutual care and protection, compassion, empathy, respect and trust derive from social practices and not from some transcendent source.

But there is nothing incompatible about these two sources of higher morality, in fact they reinforce each other. Individuals who, of necessity, are firmly anchored in a more conventional social pathway – because of practical commitments to work, family, and so on, are just as likely to have spiritual or religious commitments which overlap with the more mundane interpersonal ethics. But the crucial point is that those who don't have religious or spiritual commitments, have access to another source of ethics and values governing their behaviour and relationships which converge with that of general altrusim – care and compassion for others based on the pragmatic sacredness of self, and mutual trust and respect in social interaction.

Along with an ethics of responsibility towards others, is a similar pro-nounced use of mutual benign control as a means of providing emotional fulfilment, inner satisfaction, and life-force energy. The emphasis here is on the mutuality of the arrangement which is an aspect of the more gen-eral reciprocity that is characteristic of social behaviour. Certain imbal-ances in power and control may be tolerated, but only for a finite period and on the understanding that other aspects of the relationship will pro-duce an approximate overall balance of control. Also the energy produced through the ritual bonding in mutual benign control cannot be underes-timated especially in relation to the emotional tenor and health of rela-tionships. This brings us to the question of basic security and emotional needs. Those in this social-benign channel (probably the majority of the population), represent a normal or healthy reponse to emotional need and strategies of control. But to say this is not to imply a narrow unifor-mity of emotional response and behaviour.

It is not to say that people in this channel are simply social conformists (although many of them may be). As I suggested in the discussion of emo-tional self-motifs, there is a wide range of behaviour (and individual movement between the extremes) that can be considered normal. But for these people generally, self-esteem and security needs are fairly balanced over time with normal increases and decreases (highs and lows) at various critical points. Again, while the individuals in this group are predominantly engaged in mutual benign control, they are not averse to using more manipulative types of control, it's just that this never becomes habitual or entrenched and routine.

The social-manipulative channel

Of course it is possible that a person's behaviour and self-identity will change as a result of life situation changes and these may be such that they become more and more reliant on manipulative strategies. If this became a settled part of their existence then they could fall into the social-manipulative channel on a long-term basis. This raises a general point about all the self-identity pathways described here. They are not eternally fixed and impermeable strata.

Of course, some individuals may remain locked into a particular stratum for their whole lives, endlessy repeating the same cycle. But its also clear that individuals may move between strata at various stages of their lives. In this respect, for example, the social manipulative channel will be comprised of both those who have moved from other pathways (and not just from the social-benign channel), as well as those who are more or less permanently set within it.

A key feature of the individuals who consistently use more manipulative means for obtaining satisfaction (particularly of the emotional kind), while remaining within a socially legitimate or acceptable frame of reference, concerns issues of basic security and self-esteem. For whatever reason these individuals have found themselves to be needy around these issues but are either unable or unwilling to employ mutual benign control to address these needs. The problem would seem to be mutuality itself. The kind of relatedness in which there is genuine equality of give and take becomes impossible or unviable for the individual if there is an enduring deficit in self-esteem and basic security. There are two possibilities for the self in this situation.

The one taken in this case is that of attempting to manipulate others as a means of pre-empting them from posing any further threat to an already weakened basic security system. The anger or resentment caused by the deficit is turned outwards towards other people. This presupposes a level of efficacy and executive capacity even though the self is lacking in basic security. The energy and concentration of effort required is more than likely fuelled by anger and aggression which continue to feed on themselves as long as the manipulation continues to achieve its aim. In fact anger and psychological aggression are very visible themes in the typical strategies employed by the social-manipulative type. Emotional blackmail of the type 'I'll withhold or withdraw my love or approval if you don't take my advice' threatens a rather vicious punishment of hate and, if a particularly vulnerable person is the target, it is aggressive and bullying as well. The shifting or dumping of guilt is also part of the manipulator's repertoire, as in 'you'll make me ill, if you refuse my request' or 'how can you be so selfish after all I've done for you'.

Other types of psychological pressure or manipulation may be exerted, such as continuous nagging or prolonged silences but they are all particularly effective because they involve close ties with family colleagues and friends that we usually want to strengthen or maintain. Along with its continued effectiveness this will reinforce the manipulator's behaviour and may well last for a whole lifetime. The effectiveness of this strategy is bolstered the more it is successful because it allows the individual to avoid the possibility of seeing the problem as *their* problem. As long as the manipulation works they can delude themselves into believing that it is other people who are to blame – a classic case of self-deception.

Only if the manipulation ceases to be effective, both in getting others to comply and (thus) in filling the void in security and self-esteem, will the individual's executive capacity – the capacity to act powerfully (although inappropriately) be undercut. Only then will the individual begin to contemplate an alternative strategy and response. In the face of an imminent collapse of action and the resulting inability to achieve inner satisfaction through (outer) manipulation of others, the individual will begin to turn inward and instead of blaming others will begin to blame themselves.

The wounded/disabled self

Of course, not all people in this channel are ex-social manipulators although becoming disempowered and accepting that this has happened, would be one way of changing pathways. It's also true that by far the most numerous in this category are those who have consciously experienced disempowerment during their lives, having been forced into this pathway by dropping out of a more powerful one. Those who already are (at birth) or who have become either physically or mentally ill or disabled are typically shunted into this pathway either on a temporary or more permanent basis.

In this sense it is a critical life event and the subsequent implications it has for the person's life situation that culminates in his or her disempowerment. For instance, becoming ill with a life-threatening or chronic illness has serious consequences for the individual's capacity to manage and control their overall current life situation. From being in control of every or most aspects their lives, they are suddenly placed in a situation in which much of this control is taken away by circumstances beyond their control. This disempowerment is accompanied by a series of emotional reactions including anger, rage, self-blame, denial, depression, jealousy, acceptance as the individual passes through different phases of the illness.

In particular self-esteem and self-confidence take a considerable battering. For instance having to be cared for often creates anxiety and a lack of self-worth in the person who has to be cared for (Fox 1996). Further, becoming ill can deprive the person of the status they once held at work or even in the family. Other people tend to treat them as if they were children that should be dictated to, because they have less control over their lives. In short, becoming ill and having the physical shortcomings which that entails, means that other people have power over you. Gone is your ability to lead 'a completely independent life, earning your own living, making your own decisions, choosing the people you wished to see. Now you may find yourself in the care of someone who, however kind and well-meaning, fits you into *their* schedule' (Fox 1996, p. 49). Of course, sometimes the power of others and the vulnerability of the ill person can be abused at a time when the ill person is not really in a position to adequately defend themselves. There are also worries about losing your job, about existing on benefits and that something may happen to the person who cares for you. In addition, depending on how long your illness lasts, you may start to fear that 'if you do not recover you will grow old with nothing to look back on, except the desert of your life' (Fox 1996, p. 63).

Of course, different individuals will respond to being chronically ill in different ways depending on the range of feelings they experience. While anger and fear dominate their emotions they are likely to adopt either a 'victim' stance or a 'martyr' stance, both of which imply a sort of defensive (if not exactly defeatist) reponse. But once the individual has begun to accept some of the physical and mental constrictions on their lives and the general loss of control over their life situation they may adopt a more positive attitude to their circumstances. They may attempt to carve out a life for themselves, given their new level of health, and even begin to regain some power and control where possible (such as over the kind of treatment they receive and the way others respond to them).

With mental illness there are many similarities with the problems encountered in physical illness such as a diminution in feelings of self-worth, problems of isolation, stigmatization and patronizing responses from others and so on. But there are differences of emphasis. Typically self-identity will be the primary focus of difficulty right from the outset because more than likely the mental illness (for example, depression or schizophrenia) will be a direct result of some problem of the self, such as confusion or anxieties about relating to self or others.

In this respect it is the woundedness of the self in the first instance that leads to other problems such as negative responses from others (both lay people and doctors). Very often the person is confused, fearful and anxious about their own identity and whether they are indeed mentally ill. In fact, such is the stigma attached to mental disorders that there is often resistance to such labelling, or to taking medication which would imply the legitmacy of the label. Thus the woundedness of the self compounds the problems of the mentally ill as compared with those of physical illness. The other problems of losing friends, isolation, infantilization, lack of control over life situation, and so on, are simply added on to the primary problem around identity, and probably exacerbate it in the process.

The anti-social/criminal pathway

The most obvious defining characteristic of this pathway can be seen in the control motifs and strategies of individuals who live out their lives (or parts of their lives) in this channel. The predominant control styles and strategies are those involving exploitation, domination and coercion (including violence) as means of acquiring compliance of others as well as obtaining material and emotional rewards and satisfactions. Here also, serious or hard manipulation holds a high profile place.

Whereas the social-manipulative control motif emphasizes softer versions of manipulation which may not exactly take the other's interests into account, they do not involve overt or ruthless exploitation. This is perhaps because the softer style of manipulation has as its object the emotional allegiances and ties of the individuals it targets. The preservation of emotional ties, of course is not best served by the use of blatant or heavy-handed coercion. In the case of the anti-social or criminal pathway the preservation of an emotional bond is not the object of control. Quite the reverse, it is raw compliance without a tie or bond that is the point – a sort of negative social relationship.

Manipulation then, denuded of social bondedness, is the stock in trade of those in this channel. Of course there are a number of different elements within this group (by far the greatest number being males) emphasizing slightly different aspects as far as control and emotion motifs are concerned. At one end of the scale we have the use of violence, threats and coercion as means of settling disputes in neighbourhood gangs, hooliganism and street violence. The use of such anti-social means is a way of responding to trouble or the opposition although such behaviour may be fashioned into a way of life based on taking control of the immediate situation and for sorting out relationships. The emotional buzz, the high adrenalin rush that accompanies such skirmishes are undeniable motivating factors in such crimes (Katz 1988).

The violence perpetrated in women abuse is of a rather different order in that this involves manipulation and control over a social relationship in which there is, or was at one time, a degree of emotional bondedness. Although the male appropriates control of the woman through violence (either physical, psychological or both), the motivating factor is not a search for an emotional high as such, but rather, an attempt to shore up inner psychological weaknesses around emotional security and self-identity. By taking control of the woman and the relationship, the male attempts to cover over insecurities and a lack of inner power by predominantly physical coercion or its threat (Horley 2000).

Career criminals, however, such as those involved in armed robbery, fraud, theft and so on, are not so much attempting to take control of a particular relationship or an immediate situation – although both of these will also be involved. Rather it can be conceived of as a grandiose appropriation of control over their lives, life chances and lifestyles in general. In particular, it represents an attempt to maintain control over their current life situation and their emergent self-narrative. Their line of business in itself being anti-social, they are also dependent on non-legitimate means such as violence, torture and terror to implement their plans and objectives.

The abyss of ultimate power

Canter (1994) has pointed out that sexually motivated crimes such as rape and sexual abuse can be understood to differ in terms of the degree of control used and the attitude of the perpetrator to the victim – whether they are seen as a person, a vehicle for the perpetrator's intentions, or as a completely depersonalized object. This seems a fruitful way of distinguishing between different sorts of violent (sexually motivated) crimes, many of which involve murder. It certainly underlines the importance of the control and emotional-motivational motifs implicit in the perpetrator's self-identity.

Among these sorts of crimes are those which seem to be completely beyond the pale of what might, in this light, be thought to be conventional crime. In this respect serial murder in which the perpetrator does not know or have any connection with the victim prior to the murder, represents ultimate power and control over other human beings. An apparently random and motiveless act on closer inspection usually involves the deliberate selection of specific victims (who stand for a certain kind of person or represent a particular group).

Even within serial murder there are variations in terms of motives, crime signatures, means of killing and ways of life of such killers, so it is difficult to generalize without reservation. Nonetheless, there are clear psychological elements that seem to figure in many of these crimes. The killer's inability to empathize with their victims is prominent among them. But this seems also to be related to the killer's experience of identity problems. Many have a fragile sense of themselves and are excessively sensitive and vulnerable to real or imagined slights or put downs.

The fragility and insecurity of personal identity has lead to a number suggestions about the motivations of serial killers. Some of these crimes have been termed 'self-esteem murders' in so far as the murderer is attempting to put right or avenge a humiliation he experienced sometime in his past and in order to regain the power lost in the incident (Hale 1998). Similarly, lack of self-worth and an absence of social recognition of their value as a person seems to be a powerful motivating factor for some serial killers. After all, the commission of an abhorrent crime is capable of creating almost instantaneous notoriety, even infamy. It may have the effect of transforming a drifting nobody into a somebody or a socially isolated loner into a 'star' criminal with very positive effects on the self-esteem of the killer.

The inability of some killers to maintain relationships not only suggests a psychological inadequacy in relation to the self but a general lack of emotional intelligence (including empathy) and social skills. In these circumstances committing apparently pointless murders becomes a response to social inadequacy, the failure to create and sustain intimacy and the fear of abandonment and rejection. By completely controlling and owning the (sometimes dead) bodies of their victims, at least for a short while, the illusion of adequacy is created. The act of murder becomes a way of exerting control and achieving a distorted sense of intimacy (Masters 1993, 1995).

Unlike many other kinds of crime, control over self and others is the centrepoint and raison d'etre of serial murder. Rather than being the means to an end it becomes the end in itself. Control is entangled with the murderer's psychology, sense of self and feelings about social life. It is the killer's need to regain control over some aspect of his mental life and feelings – an inner lack of security, esteem or inner power – that motivates him to assert ultimate control over his victim's lives.

The emergent self-narrative

The above outline of social routes or pathways the self can take is obviously a broad brush depiction. They are *social* pathways, not individual ones and thus they give the outer parameters of possibility rather than the finer details of individual experience. They are certainly not meant to be exhaustive, but merely illustrative of the circuit of influences that impinge on and continually produce and reproduce the emergent self.

There is no doubt that as individuals we have a good deal of influence over the fashioning of our personal identity. We constantly try to make of ourselves what we would wish. We grapple with issues about what kind of person we are, what we should become and how we should live our lives (with zest, generosity and hope or despair, fear and anxiety). But we don't do this on our own, through thought and free action in a vacuum, so to speak. We do this always through the medium of lived experience with its attendant problems, critical events and existential dilemmas.

These provide constraints on what is possible and what we are capable of doing, as well as enabling us to take advantage of whatever opportunities may arise. The mediating influence of the social environment and the experiences we undergo should not be forgotten when we consider the emergent narrative of the self. Certainly social ties and relationships may be regarded as resources for the enhancement and creation of identity resources that may be co-opted in a positive manner. But the same relationships can also prove to be a troublesome threat or burden to our aspirations. Events, critical problems, unforseen circumstances that are essentially beyond our control, may thwart our ambitions despite our freedom to contruct our unique responses to them.

The same considerations are pertinent to the issue of what it is we refer to (or what we should be referring to), when we speak of the self-narrative. As I mentioned at the begining of this chapter, confining the concept to the stories that individuals tell themselves about themselves and their lives is to underestimate the human propensity for self-deception and self-aggrandisement. At the same time it underplays the limits that social circumstances and lived experience place on the construction of self-identity. Such a notion of self-narrative also constantly supports the illusion of the boundless freedom of human agency. Undoubtedly human individuals are self-reflexive beings and each of us desires to be a particular kind of person and to see ourselves in a certain light. But what we would wish to be, and what we actually are, do not always coincide because inescapably the social world itself plays a part in conditioning the choices we make. Of course, we do make things happen for ourselves and we can make a difference to our circumstances. But the extent to which we are able to do so is severely circumscribed by our particular social circumstances and current life situation. We cannot simply renew and revise our self-identity at will and unhindered by our surrounding social environment.

What then is the nature of the self as it undergoes and emerges from this circuit of influences? The self is a phenomenon of feeling as much as anything else. It is not an empty reflexive project. It has emotional ballast which firmly locks it into ongoing networks of social ties bonds and relationships which condition its revisability. That is why the narrative is an *emergent*, not a free-floating reflexive project or a freely revisable narrative. It is an emergent from the dialectical interplay between subjective desire and the currently unfolding life situation.

The self's heavy emotional freight of motivation and desire is the both the medium and outcome of a struggle of emotional neediness versus the harsh realities of experience and the ability to control one's current life situation. Sometimes it just doesn't work out. Illness, misfortune, disappointment, lack of social learning, or social skills, a deficit of love and approval may all conspire to rob a person not only of the texture of their lives, but their power to be who they most want to be.

Emotionally driven motives, power and control are all directly involved in day-to-day conduct and are interlinked in the continual emergence and re-emergence of self-identity. It is a mistake to think of human conduct and social identity as simply the product of reflexive monitoring and the rationalization of conduct. The human self is not a dry, thinking and surveillance machine. It is an active, feeling organism shot through with desire and neediness. Its (subjective) resilience is forever being tested against whatever the social world places in its path.

Chapter Summary

- Self-identity and self-realization are best understood as a real (rather than imagined) storyline that emerges out of the interaction between a person's agency (including their inquisitiveness and creativity) and the life experiences and social circumstances which shape and influence the trajectory of the self. This view of self-identity is set against that which envisages it as endlessly revisable or renewable, as if there was no need for proper social anchoring or validation.
- As a unifying centre of awareness, a nexus of emotional needs and desires and a focus of executive self-competence, efficacy and personal control, self-identity (in good mental health) is fairly robust and relatively durable.

- Self-identity emerges from a circuit of social and psychological influences including psychobiography, current life situation (from the individual's point of view an emotionally charged network of relationships), critical life events, existential dilemmas and problems and emotional and control motifs.
- This circuit of influences combines to channel self-identity into one of six recognizable social pathways (between which it is possible for individuals to be mobile). The pathways are: higher or spiritual; socially-benign; socially-manipulative; wounded or disabled; anti-social or criminal; ultimate power. These are broad channels or parameters within which individual self-identities are formed, but the pathways themselves must not be confused with unique self-identities.
- There are two distinct types of self-narrative; a) the stories we tell ourselves about who we are and the manner in which we live out our lives, and b) actual emergent narratives of the self (psychobiographies) that represent what actually happens to us as our lives unfold.

Afterword

What prompted me to write this book? Having been an academic sociologist for around 30 years, I have always been interested in the self (personal identity) and the associated problem of the relationship between the individual and society. When I first became a sociologist this was a rather 'undeveloped' area but progress was modest, steady and promising – especially as it was influenced by the pioneering work of Mead. However since then the early promise has all but disappeared.

I think the reasons for can be traced back to the emergence of certain perspectives that questioned the very existence of the self (and the individual) and their place in social analysis. One of the earliest claims in this respect was that the notion of an individual self was necessary to maintain the illusion that we (as individuals) have some control over our own destinies. This supposed ideological trick hides 'the fact' that we are simply bit-players and that the social system (society) really determines our thoughts and behaviour.

Subsequently those who call themselves poststructuralists have insisted that individual selves only 'appear' in language and discourse and that they have no real existence outside these parameters. According to these authors the idea that we have thoughts, feelings and desires that are ours as unique individuals is a mistaken and rather naive assumption. Instead we are 'created' by the discourses which assign us 'subject' positions and allow us to think in various ways about the world.

What has become known as 'discourse analysis' has established footholds in many areas of social analysis including sociology, social psychology and cultural studies spreading its core idea that individuals with their own intentions, purposes, personalities, desires and thoughts do not exist independently of the social discourses that 'speak for them'. Those who call themselves social constructionists also share this idea although they place less emphasis on the importance of language. For social constructionists, emotions, motives, reasons and intentions are not interior states of selves but exterior properties of contexts and actions. Such radical approaches suggest that practices, actions, activities and interactions rather than persons should be at the centre of analytic attention. More broadly, social constructionism endorses the view that emotions, desires, intentions and so on, are social constructs rather than aspects of individual experience and subjective mental states.

Closely allied with social constructionism is the perpective known as postmodernism which insists that the self is ephemeral, fragmented and discontinuous. We constantly recreate ourselves according to our desires and the situations into which we are placed. This is because the modern world itself has changed, having become more complex, shifting and ambiguous through the multiplication of lifestyles and life sectors. The idea that there is a coherent, core or continuous self is rejected in favour of a view of the endless recreation and revisability of the self and the narratives through which we choose to live our lives.

Of course, not everyone endorses these ideas about the self. Nevertheless, students and others new to the study of the self are often uncritically presented with such views as if they were indisputable or established fact, which is far from the case. It is also true that there have been strong criticisms of these views from noted scholars (Craib 1998, Porpora 1997) and such technical, academic argument is an important avenue for challenging their adequacy. In this book, however, I have chosen a rather different way to expose the weaknesses of these ideas and perspectives on the self.

Instead of discussing the nature of different perpectives and presenting the reader with a rather abstract and academic discussion, I have chosen to describe and flesh out in a positive and constructive manner, what I take to be an adequate alternative view of the self and self-identity. Thus I develop a view of the self as having a measure of freedom from the grip of language and discourse, while also recognizing the importance and influence of such factors. This 'realistic' view of personal identity stresses that it is not simply a social construct, but has a definite, individual and subjective existence partly independent of social forces.

A focus on personal identity can never be replaced or substituted by the analysis of social activities or practices. The individual person with a vibrant subjective interior must have a central place in social analysis alongside and in conjunction with social forces and factors. To imagine otherwise is a form of intellectual laziness, not to say explanatory suicide. Similarly to view self-identity as an endless self-creation or revisable narrative is both naive and misplaced. Such a view does considerable disservice to individual capabilities while at the same time, and with considerable irony, it drastically underestimates the formative influence of social forces.

There is certainly nothing fixed, static or essentialist about self-identity. A person's identity may change in accordance with social situations and circumstances (particularly their current life situation) as well as their own choices and decisions. However, this is not an endless recreation or revision of identity nor is it achieved unhindered by social forces. Important transformations in self-identity, when and if they occur, tend to be gradual rather than total, while minor changes are more frequent but essentially cosmetic. It is also possible to have a core self that underpins and co-ordinates the performances of several other social personae. But these are not different selves they are simply different facets of the same individual.

Emotion and desire are important features of personal identity, but again they are never purely social constructs. To grasp their importance for self-identity – and the way social forces are reshaped and re-channelled in the process – it is crucial to understand emotions as expressions of a person's psyche – of their unique, subjective view of their world and experience. But many approaches to the self persist in treating it as primarily cognitive (an information processing unit) and thus minimize the importance of emotion or treat it as an unusual or non-routine feature of behaviour. This view needs to be turned on its head. Self-identity is suffused with feeling and emotion even if individuals attempt to supress or stifle their expression. Emotion is the foundation on which every facet of human behaviour ultimately rests. All our intentions and purposes are coloured by it, especially our attempts to control and influence others. As I outline it in this book, self-identity, emotion and desire are delicately interwoven with interpersonal control as the means through which our desires, purposes and interests are secured. In particular, I argue that much of our behaviour relies on the benign control of others as a way of satifying emotional needs in ourselves as well as other people.

Here the whole thrust of my view of self-identity goes against the postmodern ('radical', constructionist) currents of thought which see it as an offshoot and reflection of wider discourses and other social forces. Contrary to these constructionist currents, individual private worlds and personal feelings must be grasped as central to our social experience. They must be incorporated into our understanding of the way in which self-identity and personal agency help to form and inform our social relationships and experiences.

The extensive current literature on self-help, self-development and tranformation are sensitive barometers of the age in which we live and yet the ideas to which it gives expression cannot be understood in terms of social constructionism or postmodernism. The idea of a spiritual side to the self and that inner power is a crucial ingredient in self-development needs to be registered and counterposed to postmodern currents of thought.

Existential questions about personal and social experience and the problems and dilemmas we experience as part of our everyday relationships are conspicuously absent from postmodern and constructionist analyses. The practical dynamics of encounters and relationships and the personal experiences and feelings they generate (love, hate, admiration, shame, pity, euphoria, depression and so on), are impossible to grasp if we view self-identity as some kind of behaviouristic outcome of social processes. The very essence of personal experience is obliterated by understanding it exclusively in terms of social discourses.

I first began thinking and formulating the ideas about personal identity offered in the rest of this book while I was writing a book entitled *Modern Social Theory* (1997) in which I outline what I call 'the theory of social domains'. The book develops the idea that social reality is made up of several interconnecting but partly independent domains that have their own characteristics and properties but which also intimately influence each other. One of these domains, psychobiography, portrays the self as partly independent of social forces while at the same time subject to a good deal of social influence. In one sense this present work can be understood as an extended reflection on, and elaboration of, the psychobiographical domain but without all the technical theoretical discussion in the previous book.

The theory of social domains lies in the deep background of this present work affirming rather than denying individual subjectivity and the 'inner life' of human desire and emotion. In fact, the theory of social domains celebrates the reality of this inner psychic experience and treats it as indispensable to an adequate account of modern existence. As a backdrop domain theory is also present in the idea of a dialectical interplay between real, relatively independent individuals and the social activities, settings and contexts which form their social environment. In short it understands social forces not as determiners of personal identity or individual experience, but as conditioning influences on the intentions, purposes desires and ambitions of real individuals with real self-identities.

References

Ashner, L. and Meyerson, M. 1997. *When Enough is Enough*. Dorset: Element.

Becker, E. 1974. *Revolution in Psychiatry*. New York: Free Press.

Bernstein, B. 1973. *Class, Codes and Control*, Vol. 1. London: Paladin.

Branden, N. 1985. *Honouring The Self*. New York: Bantam.

Bugliosi, V. and Gentry, C. 1977. *Helter Skelter*. Harmondsworth: Penguin.

Canter, D. 1994. *Criminal Shadows*. London: Harper Collins.

Chopra, D. 1996. *The Seven Spiritual Laws of Success*. London: Bantam.

Cohen, S. and Taylor, L. 1976. *Escape Attempts*. Harmondsworth: Penguin.

Craib, I. 1998. *Experiencing Identity*. London: Sage.

Crespi, F. 1992. *Social Action and Power*. Oxford: Blackwell.

Denscombe, M. 2001. 'Uncertain identities and health risking behaviour: the case of young people and smoking in late modernity', *British Journal of Sociology*, 52 (1): 157–77.

Dyer, W. 1979. *Pulling Your Own Strings*. Feltham: Hamlyn.

Dyer, W. 1998. *Manifest Your Destiny* London: Thorsons.

Franks, D. 1974. 'Current conceptions of competency motivation', in Field, D. (ed.), *Social Psychology for Sociologists*. London: Nelson.

Fox. J. 1996. *Surviving ME*. London: Vermillion.

Gardner, H. 1983. *Frames of Mind*. London: Harper Collins.

Giddens, A. 1984. *The Constitution of Society*. Oxford: Polity.

Giddens, A. 1991. *Modernity and Self-identity*. Oxford: Polity.

Gilbert, P. 1992. *Depression: The Evolution of Powerlessness*. New York: Guildford Press.

Goffman, E. 1959. *The Presentation of Self in Everyday Life*. New York: Doubleday.

Goffman, E. 1967. *Interaction Ritual*. New York: Anchor.

Goffman, E. 1983. 'The interaction order', *American Sociological Review*, 48. 1–17.

Goleman, D. 1996. *Emotional Intelligence*. London: Bloomsbury.

Hale, R. 1988. 'The application of learning theory to serial murder', in Holmes, R. and Holmes, S. (eds), *Contemporary Perspectives on Serial Murder*. Thousand Oaks, CA: Sage.

Heidegger, M. 1962. *Being and Time*. Oxford: Blackwell.

Hochschild, A. 1983. *The Managed Heart*. Berkeley: University of California Press.

Horley, S. 2000. *The Charm Syndrome*. London: Refuge.

Jeffers, S. 1987. *Feel The Fear and Do It Anyway*. London: Arrow.

Katz, J. 1988. *Seductions of Crime*. New York: Basic Books.

Laing, R. 1969. *The Divided Self*. Harmondsworth: Penguin.

Layder, D. 1993. *New Strategies in Social Research*. Oxford: Polity.

Layder, D. 1997. *Modern Social Theory: Key Debates and New Directions*. London: University College London Press.

Maslow, A. 1968 (1999, 3rd ed). *Towards a Psychology of Being*. New York: Wiley.

Masters, B. 1993. *The Shrine of Jeffrey Dahmer*. London: Coronet.

Masters, B. 1995. *Killing for Company*. London: Arrow.

Mead, G. 1967. *Mind, Self and Society* Chicago: Chicago University Press.

Parsons, T. 1951. *The Social System*. London: Routledge.

Porpora, D. 1997. 'The caterpillar's question: contesting anti-humanism's contestations', *Journal for the Theory of Social Behaviour*, 243–63.

Redfield, J. and Adrienne, C. 1995. *The Celestine Prophecy: An Experiential Guide*. London: Bantam.

Rogers, C. 1998 (1961). *On Becoming a Person*. London: Constable.

Roman, S. 1986. *Personal Power Through Awareness*. Tiburon: Kramer.

Rowe, D. 1988. *The Succesful Self*. London: Fontana/Collins.

Sartre, J.-P. 1966. *Being and Nothingness*. London: Methuen.

Scheff, T. 1990. *Microsociology*. Chicago: University of Chicago Press.

Stebbins, R. 1970 'Career: the subjective approach.' *Sociological Quarterly*, 11. 32–49.

Tannen, D. 1987. *That's Not What I Meant*. London: Dent.

Tannen, D. 1992. *You Just Don't Understand*. London: Virago.

Tolle, E. 2001. *The Power of Now*. London: Hodder and Stoughton.

Turner, J. 1988. *A Theory of Social Interaction*. Oxford: Polity.

Watts, A. 1962. *The Way of Zen*. Harmondsworth: Penguin.

Wrong, D. 1967. 'The oversocialized concept of man in modern sociology', in Coser, L. and Rosenberg, B. (eds), *Sociological Theory: A Book of Readings*. London: Collier Macmillan.

Index